Managing Partner 101

A Guide to Successful Law Firm Leadership

Second Edition

Lawrence G. Green

Defending Liberty
Pursuing Justice

Law Practice Management Section

Commitment to Quality: The Law Practice Management Section is committed to quality in our publications. Our authors are experienced practitioners in their fields. Prior to publication, the contents of all our books are rigorously reviewed by experts to ensure the highest quality product and presentation. Because we are committed to serving our readers' needs, we welcome your feedback on how we can improve future editions of this book. We invite you to fill out and return the comment card at the back of this book.

Cover design by Hope Morawski.

Nothing contained in this book is to be considered as the rendering of legal advice for specific cases, and readers are responsible for obtaining such advice from their own legal counsel. This book and any forms and agreements herein are intended for educational and informational purposes only.

The Section of Law Practice Management, American Bar Association, offers an educational program for lawyers in practice. Books and other materials are published in furtherance of that program. Authors and editors of publications may express their own legal interpretations and opinions, which are not necessarily those of either the American Bar Association or the Section of Law Practice Management unless adopted pursuant to the by-laws of the Association. The opinions expressed do not reflect in any way a position of the Section or the American Bar Association.

Library of Congress Catalog Card Number 00-135867
ISBN 1-57073-905-6

10 09 08 07 06   6 5 4 3 2

Discounts are available for books ordered in bulk. Special consideration is given to state bars, CLE programs, and other bar-related organizations. Inquire at Book Publishing, American Bar Association, 750 N. Lake Shore Drive, Chicago, Illinois 60611.

Dedication

To my family

and

To my colleagues

Contents

ı

Foreword

This is an important work. Much more than a "how to" book, this volume articulates a series of concepts and philosophies that are the underpinnings of a successful law firm.

One of the themes of this book is that law firms have a continuing obligation to educate and train their lawyers. The education and training relates not only to the nuts and bolts of the practice of law, but extends to the inculcation of high levels of ethical standards. Firms need to devote substantial time to this effort. This is non-billable time, but time that must nevertheless be spent if the firm desires to be successful in the long run.

Another theme of this book is that firms need to treat people with dignity and respect. The human resources of a firm represent its most significant asset. A firm needs to demonstrate this respect not only in the way partners treat associates and staff within the walls of the firm, but also by recognizing the entitlement of associates and staff to lead lives outside of the firm.

A third theme permeating the volume is the importance of following not only high standards of legal ethics, but also high standards of business ethics in a firm's dealings with its clients. Adherence to legal ethical standards is necessary but not sufficient, as the Rules of Professional Conduct do not address a number of areas. Firms must treat their clients fairly if they are to retain those clients, and what constitutes fair treatment is often defined by business ethics.

In addition to articulating these and other basic but important themes, this book is also a "how to" book. The volume includes a number of intelligent discussions of such subjects as how a managing partner should work with practice groups and committees, set firm-wide and individual goals, and deal with problem situations. In addition, a number of very creative programs are discussed, including a sabbatical program, a case presentation program, and a client roundtable program.

The book very much reflects the type of person the author is. I have had the privilege of working with Larry Green for the past twelve years. I first came to know Larry when I became faculty director of the Root-Tilden Scholarship Program at New York University School of Law, and continued to work closely with him once I became Dean of the Law School. We at NYU Law view ourselves as a community that includes not only our students and faculty, but also our alumni. A 1977 graduate of NYU Law and a Root-Tilden Scholar himself, Larry has been very active in alumni affairs, serving on the Alumni Council of the Root-Tilden Program and as President of the NYU Law Alumni of New England. In these roles, he has provided much welcome advice, reflecting perceptive insight, sound judgment, and great sensitivity.

Especially in an era when law practice has become more competitive and when lawyers have expressed increasing concern about "quality of life" issues, there are lessons to be learned in this book by managing partners of firms of all sizes. Indeed, I hope that this book will be widely read and discussed, as it will ultimately serve to the benefit of the hundreds of thousands of persons who work at law firms and the millions of clients they serve.

> John Sexton
> Dean, New York University School of Law
> New York, New York

Preface

I have not been the ideal managing partner, and ours is not the perfect law firm. Yet in looking back over my tenure as managing partner, I take a great deal of pride in my accomplishments and our firm's progress.

While our firm has increased the depth and scope of our services over the years, I am most proud of how fair we have been to our lawyers, staff, and clients. Ours is a humane firm; we respect the dignity of each individual who works here and the rights of each client.

I am writing this a year after relinquishing my managerial responsibilities, having decided to devote more time to my practice, family, and outside interests. Given the amount of time and attention I have spent over the past decade as a managing partner, I wish to share some of the lessons I have learned, in the hope that my experience will benefit other lawyers and their firms.

I do not claim to have all the answers. I do not presume that my answers are the only means for achieving certain goals. I can state with some confidence, however, what I believe does and does not work, as I have experienced a great deal during my tenure. I was elected managing partner amidst a very difficult time at our firm.

One of our firm's five founding partners had passed away very suddenly the previous year, and we proceeded to lose three of the remaining four founding partners over the next two. I was then our firm's youngest partner, and I could have taken this opportunity to move to another firm. Yet I decided to pick up the pieces and rebuild our firm with my remaining six partners.

We began as a firm of fifteen lawyers whose ranks had been decimated, with the partners on the hook for some significant financial obligations. Over the next decade, we experienced two mergers, both involving the integration of smaller "boutique" specialty practices into our firm. We underwent an office space relocation to a better building with a more favorable lease and the start of a branch office in Washington, D.C. Along the way, we recruited and promoted many talented lawyers and staff. When I stepped down from my position, we were a firm of fifty lawyers practicing in a variety of specialties. A few months later, a firm of twenty-five lawyers in a neighboring state approached our firm about the possibility of a merger. My successor asked me to lead the effort to consider and ultimately effectuate this merger. Sufficient time has now elapsed to declare this merger a success.

Today, we are a firm of eighty lawyers, with offices in Boston, Providence, and Washington, D.C., a firm whose best days are ahead. And as our firm's managing partner, I have experienced a fascinating personal odyssey, learning a great deal in the process.

This text is not a tell-all, behind-the-scenes story of our firm's history. Although such an account would no doubt prove to be an interesting read, my respect for the privacy of my colleagues and confidences of our firm clearly preclude such an account.

My intent is to describe what has worked for me as a managing partner and for our firm. Many of my insights are premised upon nothing more than common sense and decency. Although such concepts should be obvious, unfortunately all too many firms pay insufficient attention to these notions. As a result, they shortchange their employees and clients, and ultimately, themselves. The humane law firm need not be an oxymoron. By raising the bar of the standards it sets for the treatment of employees and clients, the firm will enhance its ability to achieve success.

I hope to share some insights with present and future managing partners, so that they, in turn, may adopt and adapt a few ideas to improve their own firms. Perhaps the discussions and actions that this volume may prompt will serve to benefit the overall legal profession.

Acknowledgments

I wish to express my appreciation to a number of people for their contributions, direct and indirect, to this book.

I am very grateful to the American Bar Association Law Practice Management Section Publishing Board, including in particular Beverly Loder, Judith Grubner, Linda Ravdin, and Tim Johnson. I am also grateful to the ABA reviewers and editors, including Jeffrey Flax, Sean Flynn, Howard Hatoff and Arthur Greene.

The original edition of *Managing Partner 101* was published by the ABA Section of Law Practice Management in 1990. Several chapters of my volume were influenced by that work.

John Sexton, Dean of New York University School of Law, has been both a good friend and a role model. I very much appreciate his words of encouragement as I worked on this project.

Several of my colleagues provided very helpful comments. In this connection, I thank Jim Hamilton, Marianne Sadowski and Paula Berg. I also wish to thank my secretary, Kathleen Kelly, for her generous assistance.

More generally, I thank all of my colleagues, past and present. Just as it is said that a teacher learns from his or her students, I as a managing partner learned a great deal from the partners, associates and staff members with whom I have had the privilege of working over the years.

Finally, I wish to express my gratitude and love to my family, immediate and extended. To my parents, David and Phyllis Green, who have been a constant source of strength and support over the years. To my grandfather, Morris Berson, with whom I "walked the halls" as a young boy and saw the respect and admiration he had of his employees. And to Paula, Adam, and Nat for their love, patience, and understanding.

Preamble:
The Four Cornerstones of
a Successful Law Firm

A law firm's success is not simply a function of its won-lose percentage on cases. Nor is a law firm's success merely a function of its profitability.

A firm can be successful at any size. Increased size may often result in higher profits; yet the increase in size may also diminish a firm's working atmosphere.

There are four cornerstones of a successful law firm. A firm must:

1. *Provide its clients with quality legal product and service within its areas of expertise.*
2. *Provide its lawyers and staff with a healthy working environment.*
3. *Adhere to high standards of legal and business ethics.*
4. *Be financially sound.*

Until a firm excels in all four areas, it cannot deem itself successful—simply put, three out of four does not cut it.

A firm that excels in quality product and service, as well as in a healthy working environment and profitability, is not successful if it falls short in its compliance with ethical standards. And ultimately, ethical corner cutting will hurt the firm in the other three categories

—as honest lawyers and staff will not wish to remain over the long run.

A firm that places overly excessive demands upon its personnel may be practicing quality law—achieving substantial profitability and adhering to high ethical standards—but at a significant cost if the working atmosphere precludes lawyers and staff from properly enjoying a life outside the firm. How can a firm be successful if lawyers and staff are unhappy because of excessive job demands?

A firm that excels in a healthy work environment, ethical adherence, and profitability will not be successful if it cannot provide quality legal product and service. In the long run, the clients will go elsewhere, and so will the better lawyers and staff members.

And a firm that does well in terms of quality product and service, a healthy working atmosphere, and ethical compliance cannot be successful if it is not financially sound. The competitive forces are just too great to allow such a firm to attract and retain those lawyers and support staff required to maintain excellence in the other three areas.

Quality of Product/Quality of Service

The quality of a law firm's product is a function of the lawyers' and staff's skills, expertise, diligence, and attention to detail. Lawyers are motivated, indeed required, to provide a high quality product to properly represent their clients' needs. Judges and members of the bar review lawyers' product, and product of poor quality will certainly not improve lawyers' reputations. Although individual lawyers are already motivated to provide a quality product, a firm must adopt and enforce numerous internal procedures to ensure that it achieves quality.

A firm must make sure that its lawyers keep up with developments in their respective fields of law by attending continuing legal education programs and reading relevant publications. Because the law is so complex, it is also necessary to establish an expertise policy, so that certain lawyers are designated as experts in given areas of the law. To obtain designation as an expert, a lawyer must have a sufficient amount of experience in the practice area, keep up with area developments, and regularly attend department meetings.

To further promote high standards for quality product, a firm must also establish a system for properly training its more junior lawyers. This requires a substantial time commitment, often not properly billable, on the part of more senior lawyers. Quality product also depends upon the work of the support staff, who must be trained to produce quality work and made to understand why such quality work is important.

It is equally crucial to stress the quality of the law firm's service to its clients. Quality of service is a function of communication, responsiveness, and timeliness. These abilities are unfortunately not sufficiently recognized at many firms. Yet what good is the beautifully drafted contract if it does not refer to a key issue, which the lawyer failed to learn from his or her client? And what good is the perfectly drafted prejudgment attachment motion if it is filed one day after another creditor has attached the same assets?

More than anything else, quality service requires a full understanding of the client's needs in the context of the bigger picture. It is not enough for a lawyer to simply listen to what his or her client has to say. A lawyer must probe his or her client to review possible contingencies and alternatives. This communication process takes place at the outset of the representation, but does not stop there. Quality service requires regular and frequent communication with the client, as changes may take place in the legal and factual context of the case, and otherwise in response to the actions of opposing counsel.

Apart from communication, quality service requires responsiveness and timeliness. Sometimes it is not good enough to do your best when responding to such changes. Sometimes circumstances require the lawyer to do whatever it takes—obviously within the bounds of applicable ethical principles—to protect the client's interests.

Working Atmosphere

Too many firms pay insufficient attention to the working atmosphere they provide for their personnel. A firm's working environment is based in part upon tangible elements: the quality of the space, office layout, library, and computer and telecommunications systems. Although these elements are important, the firm's "intangible infrastructure." is of much greater significance to defining a healthy work environment.

The intangible infrastructure of a firm consists of its policies, programs, and overall culture. To ensure that these components are coming together to form a healthy intangible infrastructure, four basic principles must be recognized.

1. *Law firms and their personnel must understand that serving their clients is their most important duty;* it is not to maximize profits. If a firm provides quality legal product and service, profits will follow. A firm's overall culture should not be premised upon monetary considerations. It should be premised upon serving clients.

2. *A firm must pay attention to the needs of its personnel,* and this requires recognizing that lawyers and staff have lives beyond the firm. The expectations that a firm establishes for its partners, associates, and staff must respect the right of the individual to have and enjoy a personal life.

3. *Every rule and regulation must have a supporting rationale,* and the rule, as well as the rationale, must be understood by all personnel. The underlying rationale may be based upon a number of factors—quality service, ethical standards, common courtesy, or just plain common sense. Compliance with any rule will be enhanced if the firm's personnel understand the basis for each and every rule.

4. *People deserve to be treated with respect and dignity.* Law firms are already sufficiently tiered so that junior partners, associates, paralegals, and secretaries do not need added reminders of their respective places. We are all human beings, and we are all working toward the same goal: to provide quality legal services to our clients.

Ethical Compliance

All lawyers are required to adhere to the *Rules of Professional Conduct,* which sets forth canons and rules in clear, explicit terms. To the extent that there is some gray area in interpreting the rules, there are numerous authorities—court decisions, administrative rulings, and published treatises—that provide significant guidance to the lawyer.

Equally important is a firm's adherence to a high level of business ethics. While most law firms do a good job in ensuring that their lawyers comply with their legal ethical obligations, the bar's overall adherence to high standards of business ethics is not as consistent. The legal ethical standards only go so far, and it is imperative that a lawyer practices sound business ethics if he or she is to properly serve the client.

Unlike the legal ethical standards, which are for the most part neatly published and annotated, business ethical standards are not always found in any one place. They may be best found in our internal sense of right and wrong.

For example, when a lawyer first meets with a prospective client, it is important that the lawyer not oversell what he or she can accomplish for that client. The legal ethical standards are silent on this issue. Unfortunately, there are lawyers who exaggerate what they can accomplish. In such a case, it is business ethics that must be invoked to ensure that a lawyer does not overpromise a prospective client.

In a similar instance, the legal ethical standards prohibit lawyers from charging "clearly excessive" fees, yet these standards do not adequately address the need, for instance, to comply with the client's budgetary constraints. The legal ethical principles do not otherwise recognize that a bill may need to be discounted in fairness to a client, even when the charge is not clearly excessive. Once again, it is business ethics, and not legal ethics, that must be invoked.

Legal ethical standards set forth a series of definitive rules with respect to conflicts of interest. We know that, as a general rule, we cannot represent clients with adverse interests in a litigation or on opposite ends of a business transaction. Legal ethical standards do not address, however, the issue of representing business competitors in separate matters. Certainly it is commonplace for firms to represent more than one banking institution or insurance company on separate matters. Should a firm assume representation for two different business competitors if achieving a successful result for one could disadvantage the other? The legal ethical standards are also silent on this point. Business ethical standards should come into play and preclude a firm from taking on both representations.

One of management's tasks is to make sure that the firm attracts honorable lawyers with high ethical standards. Another task of management is to inculcate a sense of commitment to high ethical standards among lawyers and staff. The message must be communicated and constantly reinforced: if something does not smell right, or if there is any doubt whatsoever, staff and lawyers must report the matter to the managing partner or partner charged with ethical compliance. Those in charge of handling ethical compliance must make it clear that there will be no repercussions whatsoever arising from such a report.

Financial Soundness

Published materials on law firm profitability abound. And there is certainly no lack of emphasis on profitability at most firms.

Yet the real issue is not profitability but rather the overall financial soundness of the firm. Obviously profitability is important, because poor profitability may hinder a firm's efforts to attract and retain good people. Yet capital and debt structure, the partners' individual responsibility for firm obligations, and the firm's "functional stability" also define a firm's financial soundness.

First, a few words about profitability. A firm's profitability must be viewed on the "micro" level and not on the "macro" level. Statistical surveys of overall profitability, or even per partner profitability, are not terribly enlightening. For example, Firm A may have a higher per partner profit than Firm B, but Firm B's lower figure might reflect the fact that it is doing a better job in promoting associates to partners, presumably a sign of financial health. If Firm A is maintaining a higher figure because it is not doing as good a job in promoting its associates, it can not be viewed as the more financially sound of the two.

Keep in mind that the overall profitability of a firm does not tell you what each partner is paid. If the distribution of profits is not equitable, the profitability realized by at least some partners is insufficient. Accordingly, a firm must review profitability on the micro level, which means considering the take-home compensation of each individual partner in the context of his or her contributions to the firm.

A financially sound firm has a capital and debt structure that does not cause its partners to lose sleep at night. The amount of the firm's capital will depend upon its income and expense patterns but should be at least sufficient to cover the possibility of a prolonged dry spell. A firm's debt per partner should not be excessive, and the guaranty obligations of individual partners should not be burdensome. A financially sound firm has assets with a liquidation value substantially in excess of debt obligations. A financially sound firm does not have inadequate levels of malpractice insurance or substantially unfunded retirement obligations.

By "functional stability," I refer to a situation in which the firm does not rely unduly upon any one lawyer or any one client in terms of percentage of gross revenue. The functionally stable firm can afford to lose any one lawyer and any one client and still be fully viable. Obviously, it is more difficult for very small firms to survive the loss of a key partner, but partners of such firms have the ability to become closer to one another personally and professionally, the need to build trust among themselves.

In sum, the issue is not profitability on a macro level but overall financial soundness, measured by profitability on the micro level, the fairness of the division of profits, the adequacy of the firm's capital, the low level of debt, the absence of onerous guaranty obligations, and the functional stability of the firm. Ultimately, it is a question of the collective peace of mind of the firm's partners.

These four cornerstones are the reference points for the managing partner in his/her efforts to build the successful law firm. The chapters that follow are intended to provide a guide for the managing partner in undertaking this effort.

PART I

A Leadership Guide for the Managing Partner

The Job Description 1

Managing partners spend a great deal of time defining and refining the job descriptions of their underlings—and this is important. Yet it is even more crucial to have a defined job description for the managing partner—and it is equally important that all partners agree on this job description. If there is no job description, the managing partner should create one and quickly obtain partnership approval thereof. The managing partner's position is far too crucial to the firm's well-being to allow for any confusion. Ideally, a managing partner's job description is set forth in the firm's partnership agreement, the constitution of the firm. Alternatively, there should be a partnership vote—reflected in the minutes of the firm—defining job responsibilities.

The managing partner's job description should also be detailed in the firm's employee handbook—if not in its entirety, at least in summary form—so that there is no confusion on the part of associates and staff as to the managing partner's role. Although the nature and scope of the managing partner's position will depend upon a firm's size, traditions, and culture, the managing partner of any law firm should undertake the following responsibilities.

Developing and Implementing the Firm's Strategic Plan

When developing a strategic or long-range plan, a firm's managing partner must take the lead and obtain full partnership support for such a plan. The managing partner should also oversee the plan's implementation and monitor the firm's progress in achieving the goals of that plan. The managing partner should also work with individual partners and administrative directors to help them establish their own long-term goals in coordination with the firm's goals. (The subjects of the strategic plan and goal-setting are discussed in Chapters 2 and 3.)

Managing the Firm

The managing partner serves as the firm's chief executive officer. Although ultimate authority rests with the partner, the managing partner is responsible for the firm's overall management. Such overall management encompasses the following responsibilities. The managing partner:

1. *Coordinates the firm's practice among its practice groups.* The managing partner, in coordination with the chairs of practice groups, ensures that services are rendered in a professional, ethical, timely, and economic manner, and that the firm is providing the requisite support to the lawyers within each practice group. (This subject is addressed more comprehensively in Chapter 10.)
2. *Oversees the firm's committees.* The managing partner oversees the work of the firm's committees and coordinates the tasks to be performed and the timetable of the committees' work with committee chairs. (See Chapter 9.)
3. *Supervises the firm's administrative directors.* Essential to the proper functioning of a law firm are dedicated and talented administrative, financial, and human resource directors. The managing partner must meet regularly with these

people to supervise and coordinate their work, and to be kept apprised of developments within the firm.

4. *Meets with the associates and support staff of the firm.* The managing partner meets regularly with the firm's associates and support staff to review workplace developments—including additions to personnel and changes of policy—and to answer questions and address concerns. (The firm's treatment of these important groups of human resources is discussed in Chapters 13 and 14.)

5. *Promulgates and oversees compliance with firm policies and procedures.* A firm's culture is substantially defined by the rationality of its policies and procedures, and the fairness with which they are enforced. The managing partner is responsible for the promulgation and enforcement of firm policies and procedures. (Chapter 11 addresses this area more comprehensively.)

6. *Monitors the firm's financial performance.* The managing partner is responsible for monitoring the firm's financial performance, both on the revenue side, including oversight of time posted, bills rendered, and accounts receivable, and on the expense side, including budgetary compliance and approval of non-budgeted expenses. The managing partner is also responsible for ensuring the overall financial soundness of the firm, by addressing the firm's capital and debt structure, malpractice coverage, retirement obligations, and other long-term obligations.

7. *Ensures the firm's compliance with ethical standards.* The managing partner is fluent in the applicable ethical standards and arranges for the training of lawyers and staff to ensure compliance with these standards. In this context, Rules 5.1, 5.2, and 5.3 of the *ABA Model Rules of Professional Conduct* have special significance. Adopted in virtually all jurisdictions, these rules stipulate that partners are responsible for lawyers and non-lawyers acting under their supervision. Partners must also make efforts to guarantee that the firm establishes measures that ensure that subordinates act in conformity with the *Rules of Professional Conduct.*

8. *Oversees the hiring and orientation of new personnel:* The managing partner is responsible for overseeing the firm's recruitment, interviewing, and hiring practices, and orientation of new personnel.

9. *Oversees the evaluation and professional development of personnel.* The managing partner is responsible for overseeing the training, mentoring, and review of all personnel, and the professional development and promotion of individual lawyers and staff members. The managing partner is also responsible for supervising the termination of personnel.

10. *Monitors the infrastructure of the firm.* The managing partner is responsible for the efficient use and effective operation of the firm's infrastructure, which includes its space, library, facilities, and telecommunication and computer systems.

11. *Oversees the firm's marketing program.* The managing partner is responsible for supervising the firm's marketing program, especially the external aspects of the program, such as newsletters, client seminars, Web page listings, and firm brochures.

12. *Establishes the firm's calendar.* The managing partner is responsible for the firm's annual calendar and establishes dates and deadlines for annual budgets and associate reviews and coordinates various meetings for the partners, practice groups, and committees, as well as firm functions and events.

13. *Ensures compliance with legal obligations:* The managing partner ensures that the firm is in full compliance with applicable federal, state, and local legal requirements.

Governing the Firm

The managing partner is responsible for the governance of the firm, including the following:

1. *Convening and chairing partnership meetings.* The managing partner convenes partners on a regular basis and presents

for partnership consideration those matters reserved to the partners under the firm's partnership agreement.

2. *Reporting to the partners.* The managing partner regularly reports to the partners in a manner that keeps them fully apprised of the functioning of the firm.
3. *Mediating and adjudicating disputes between partners.* The managing partner mediates and, if necessary, adjudicates disputes that arise between and among partners.

Representing the Firm

The managing partner acts as the firm's representative, or ensures that an appropriate firm representative is present at important community and bar events.

Obviously one person cannot possibly perform all of these tasks, especially if that person is also a practicing lawyer serving clients. To be successful, the managing partner must coordinate with individual partners, practice heads, committee chairs, and administrative directors to ensure that all responsibilities are properly performed.

One person is ultimately responsible for the proper performance of each of the above tasks, and this person is the managing partner.

The Strategic Plan | **2**

Any business or organization needs to have a strategic or long-term plan, and law firms are no different.

When a managing partner first assumes responsibility, there should be a full review and understanding of the firm's strategic plan. This plan may be outdated and require amendment, or there may be no plan at all. In the event that no plan exists, the managing partner should work with a small committee of partners to outline a plan for partnership review. Once there is consensus on an overall outline, the managing partner may then proceed to formalize the plan for ultimate approval by the partnership.

The strategic plan should:

1. *Articulate a vision for the firm.*
2. *Appraise the present reality of the firm.*
3. *Set forth, in detail, how to transition from the present reality to the future aspiration.*

Defining the Vision

It is critical that there be partnership consensus on a vision for the firm. A firm cannot succeed if its partners are working at cross-purposes. Thus, the managing partner must define the vision and then procure full partnership support. The vision for the firm might read as follows:

Five years from now, our firm should be a first-rate, full service [or specialty] law firm of approximately X lawyers. We should be in a position where we are recognized in our legal and business community as a successful, reputable, aggressive firm on the rise, and where we are recognized, specifically by those who know us best, as the preeminent [mid]-sized firm in our city. We should provide high quality legal service to a diverse clientele. We should provide a healthy working atmosphere for and fair compensation to our lawyers and staff. We should attract talented persons to our ranks because of our working atmosphere, compensation structure, and reputation in the community. We should comply with the highest standards of legal and business ethics.

While the full strategic plan is most likely a confidential document for the partners' eyes only, the vision for the firm is something that should be made known to the associates and staff members. Simply put, people work more productively when they understand how their jobs relate to the broader goals of the organization.

Appraising the Reality

Appraising a firm's present reality is a very delicate task, but improvement can only happen once you define what that reality is and what strengths and weaknesses exist.

A firm's reality is partially defined by numbers and statistics. These numbers might include the ratios of partners to associates in the firm's practice groups, the billable hours of partners and associates, the billings and collections of the lawyers, and the firm's realization rate of dollars collected to time charges posted. These numbers should also be compared to numbers from prior years and industry statistics of comparable firms.

Yet numbers alone cannot and should not define the full picture. An accurate appraisal of the present reality involves asking and answering a number of questions that are not defined in numerical terms.

◆ *What is the quality of legal work being provided by each of our practice groups? Are we providing first-rate legal services for our clients? How do we compare with our competition?*

◆ *Do we provide a healthy working atmosphere for our lawyers and staff? Are we attracting high quality individuals to our firm? Are we retaining our best people? What is the morale level of our personnel?*

◆ *Are we financially stable? What would happen if we lost a key client or a key partner? Do our partners seem satisfied with their level of profitability in the firm and how that profit is divided among them?*

◆ *Are we satisfied with our ethical compliance? Do we treat our clients fairly? How are we viewed in the legal and business community?*

Honestly answering these questions may become a very delicate undertaking. Yet a firm's present reality cannot be properly assessed unless these types of questions are genuinely answered. The managing partner must find a balance between candor and tact while formulating a plan to address these issues.

Transitioning from the Present Reality to the Future Aspiration

The bulk of the firm's strategic plan consists of a comprehensive and detailed series of steps defining how the firm should transition from the present reality to the future aspiration. Among the topics that may be addressed are:

- Recruiting new legal talent.
- Strengthening existing departments.
- Creating new practice groups.
- Improving the firm's mentoring and training of lawyers.
- Expanding to additional space.
- Hiring additional support personnel.
- Improving the firm's information technology systems.
- Enhancing the firm's marketing efforts.
- Setting higher goals for hours posted and bills rendered.
- Establishing more rigorous policies for accounts receivable.
- Enhancing the firm's reputation in the greater business and legal communities.

The plan should set forth timetables for accomplishing the various tasks and assign responsibility to relevant lawyers, administrators, and committee and department chairs.

The managing partner should present the plan to the partnership for approval—it is crucial to reach a unanimous or near unanimous support for the plan. The managing partner should then work in conjunction with the various personnel and committees to implement the plan by monitoring the firm's progress on at least a quarterly basis and reporting back to the partners on the firm's progress.

Establishing Individual Goals | **3**

Once the strategic plan for the firm is in place, the managing partner must work with individual staff and lawyers to define their own goals in a manner consistent with the overall goals of the firm. The confluence of individual achievements will help a firm realize its vision.

The establishment of goals by and for individuals is not an easy undertaking. If the goal is set in too lofty a manner, it will become apparent all too quickly that the goal is unreachable, resulting in discouragement and possibly abandonment. On the other hand, if the goals of individual partners are not set high enough, then there may be dissatisfaction on the part of the overall partnership at the end of the year.

Recognizing Differentials

All too often firms make the mistake of setting the same goals for all partners. Just as a good basketball team recognizes the need for role players—the playmaker, the scorer, the rebounder, the key defender—so, too, should a law firm recognize the need to ask different partners to maximize different skills. Some partners are more natural at attracting business than others. Some partners are harder workers than others; others are better supervisors of associates. Goal-setting needs to recognize these differentials.

Differentials must also recognize the realities of an individual partner's situation. A younger partner may have greater energy to post more hours than a senior partner. Yet this same younger partner may not have the as many business contacts and should not be expected to introduce as much work to the firm as a senior partner. And the partner whose home demands preclude him or her from devoting the number of hours worked by other partners should have a reasonable reduction in his or her goals—but should also have an appropriate adjustment in his or her compensation.

The One-on-One Setting of Goals

The managing partner should meet with each individual partner at the beginning of the year to review that partner's performance during that past year and discuss goals for the coming one. The partner should be asked ahead of time to consider his or her numbers from the past year, and to think about areas for development and improvement in the coming one. Numbers alone do not tell the story—client demand is essential to good numbers, and practice proficiency is essential to attracting and retaining clients. Thus, the discussion should not only address numbers but numerous other concerns. The following outline includes some of the topics the managing partner and a partner should cover:

I.   A partner's numbers.
    A.   Hours posted.
    B.   Bills rendered.
    C.   Cash receipts.
    D.   Realization rates.
    E.   Write-offs and discounts.
II. Achievements and disappointments in the partner's practice.
    A.   Successes and failures in the past year.
    B.   Level of satisfaction with the partner's own practice.

      C. Level of satisfaction with the firm's support for the partner's practice.

III. Efforts to improve the partner's practice skills.
      A. Continuing legal education reading and seminars.
      B. Bar section meetings.
      C. Developing new practice areas.
      D. Narrowing the focus of practice.
      E. Upgrading computer skills.

IV. Practice development efforts.
      A. Targeting new work from existing clients.
      B. Targeting new clients.
      C. Involvement in trade group and industry meetings.
      D. Public exposure.

V. Administrative contributions to the firm.
      A. Review of committee assignment.
      B. Contributions to practice group.
      C. Mentoring of associates.
      D. Attendance and participation at meetings.

VI. Pro bono and community activities.

These one-on-one discussions should also allow the individual partner to offer suggestions about the firm to the managing partner. The managing partner should welcome any such suggestions, and based upon these one-on-one discussions should have an increased awareness of issues to be addressed on a firm-wide basis. Ideally, the managing partner should be in a position to compile and share the goals of individual partners with all partners, which allows partners to learn more about one another's practices. In addition, partners may discover potential synergies for referrals of work and joint marketing efforts.

The managing partner should ensure that a system is established for similar one-on-one discussions to take place with all associates. The discussions should involve the managing partner, department chair, or mentor for the associate.

The managing partner should also conduct one-on-one discussions with the firm's key administrators at the beginning of the year to review each person's performance over the past year and goals for the coming one. The managing partner should encourage the administrator's suggestions for improvements within the firm and welcome those thoughts and ideas.

Monitoring Performance

Setting goals becomes meaningless unless progress is monitored. Monthly financial reports to partners should include comparisons of numerical goals to actual numbers, so that partners can see exactly where they stand in their own numbers and in relation to other partners. Peer pressure—although not necessarily verbalized—will influence those partners who falter in performance, and this is not a bad thing. When a partner is falling significantly behind, the issue is probably best addressed in a private meeting with the managing partner.

When partners are running ahead of their goals, it may be appropriate to correct their goals midyear to discourage these partners from resting on their laurels. Over the years my custom was to make such midyear corrections by increasing goals for those partners running ahead without making reductions for those running behind.

The managing partner also should create a system for monitoring associate and staff goals through department chairs, mentors, and supervisors. Associates should receive their current hours-posted figures for the month and year on a monthly basis. The managing partner, department chair, or mentor should approach any associate working considerably below goals for a particular month. The contact should be in a non-threatening manner to inquire whether a problem exists. Meetings with associates to monitor goals should otherwise occur on a quarterly or even semi-annual basis.

Ultimately, the managing partner should motivate individuals to establish goals and monitor their performance largely on their own initiative, in accordance with the standards and expectations already defined by the firm. Such self-evaluation can be a very valuable exercise.

Setting the Example | 4

The managing partner needs to invoke various techniques when leading the firm. Leadership by example is one such technique, and if done right, a most effective one. Individuals throughout the firm will look to the example set by the managing partner. The model that the managing partner sets takes on many different forms.

The Managing Partner as Practitioner

The managing partner must set the example for the standard of practice proficiency that the firm expects of its lawyers. As practitioner, the managing partner provides quality product and service for clients, actively participates in practice group discussions, and acts as a practice expertise resource within the firm. Such an example is also set by promptly returning phone calls, adhering to the firm's docketing policy, and always acting in a highly professional manner.

The Managing Partner as Partner

The managing partner is a model for other partners in the firm. The managing partner has far less credibility when addressing hours posted and accounts receivable issues if he or she is falling short of hours-posted goals (presumably a reduced goal to recognize the time spent on management) or if his or her accounts receivable are not under control. The managing partner also sets the tone for other partners' relationships with associates and staff. If the managing partner expects other partners to treat employees with dignity and respect, then the managing partner must take the lead in doing so. The managing partner should also attend all firm functions and events if partnership attendance and participation is to be promoted.

The Managing Partner as Mentor

The success of a law firm depends upon the professional development of its lawyers. Ideally, every assignment given to a junior lawyer should be viewed as an opportunity to teach. The supervising partner should take the time to frankly discuss what is expected of the lawyer and to review that lawyer's work. This is a time-consuming and often non-billable effort, yet is fundamental to the growth of the law firm. The managing partner can and should set the example for partners and generously offer his or her time to supervising associates and serving as a mentor to one or more associates within the practice group.

The Managing Partner as a Follower of Firm Policy and Procedure

If the managing partner expects to effectively enforce firm policy and procedure, then he or she must religiously follow firm policy and procedure, which means everything from posting hours on a regular and timely basis to conforming with the firm's casual attire policy. If the policy is one that the managing partner cannot adhere to, either the policy needs to be changed or the firm needs a new managing partner—others will not adhere if the managing partner is not in full compliance. Being conscientious of the firm's appearance is also important. It should not be beneath a managing partner to stoop down to pick up the stray shred of paper in the corridor.

The Managing Partner as a Contributor to the Community

Lawyers have an obligation to serve the community. All types of needs exist in any community and there are all types of ways in which lawyers can serve. For example, a managing partner can take on pro bono assignments or assist community organizations and nonprofit entities.

Managing Partner as a Human Being

Law firms should encourage their lawyers to create a healthy balance between their professional and personal lives and to be honest, well-rounded, and interesting individuals. The managing partner should set an example by demonstrating high personal values, maintaining a healthy balance between his or her professional and personal lives, and interacting with personal and professional integrity.

If the managing partner sets the example in these six areas, he or she gains greater credibility when dealing with partners, associates, and staff and may also find his or her example replicated in the actions of others. The managing partner needs to understand that others are watching for the proper model to be defined.

Learning From Losses 5

The expression "Victory has a thousand fathers, but defeat is an orphan" carries a great deal of truth in the legal world. Lawyers excel at taking credit when things go well. Yet all too often they excel at deflecting the blame when things don't go their way.

Politely put, adversity happens. What firms can and should do is to learn from their losses. The situation may be extremely delicate, involving bruised egos or, perhaps, pointing the finger at other personnel. The managing partner must make sure that defeats are properly analyzed, so that the firm and its lawyers can learn from their mistakes.

The Lost Case

It has been said that the lawyer who claims never to have lost a case has not tried enough cases. By analogy, the law firm that has never lost a case has not been around long enough. Cases are lost from time to time, yet lawyers should not casually dismiss losses by claiming that the judge or jury was wrong. Judges and juries do in fact make mistakes, but so do lawyers.

The managing partner should have a good sense of the major litigation matters being handled and trials being conducted. The managing partner, in conjunction with the trial department coordinator, should create a system for debriefing lawyers who have lost cases. This debriefing session should be conducted privately, discretely, and tactfully, but not casually. The managing partner might ask the following questions.

- *Did the lawyers prepare properly?*
- *How did the lawyers on the case perform?*
- *How did we compare with opposing counsel?*
- *How could the firm have been more supportive?*
- *What can the firm and lawyers in question learn from this defeat?*

Once these questions are answered and discussed, some discussion on how to avoid this problem in the future should be conducted. A partnership or a trial department meeting might devote itself to a post mortem. Such a session may be painful but should not be humiliating. The firm should use a lost case as a situation to teach and instruct.

The Lost Client

Senior doctors at hospitals conduct formal sessions to analyze patients' deaths. Law firms rarely have such sessions when they lose clients. They should.

Unlike the lost trial, which is difficult for the trial lawyer to conceal, the loss of a client is not always made known. The responsible lawyer may not necessarily announce a loss or may not even immediately realize that the client has been lost—the client may just fade away by simply not referring in new matters.

The managing partner should create a policy in which supervising lawyers notify the managing partner of a client loss. The firm's lawyers should be on the honor system to do so, just as they are on the honor system to bring all client fees in through the firm.

The managing partner should privately and confidentially discuss what happened with the lawyer. Perhaps it is a matter that can be rectified. A managing partner might intercede to address the client's grievance, if necessary by substituting a new supervising lawyer. Even if the matter cannot be remedied, there are lessons to be learned. If the supervising lawyer cannot provide a full explanation for the loss, the managing partner should contact the client to find out what happened. The client has already been lost, so the supervising lawyer is hardly in a position to complain about such action.

An appropriate debriefing and follow-up should also be initiated—probably at the partnership level—so that others benefit from such lessons.

The Lost Employee

The managing partner should personally communicate with all associates and staff members who give notice of their termination. During these discussions, the managing partner should inquire into the reason for the termination. Even when the reason has nothing to do with the firm, such as a geographical relocation, the managing partner can still learn something from the departing employee by asking, "Do you have any suggestions for what we should be doing differently?"

When the employee's departure has been prompted by something at the firm, there may be a good bit more to learn. Perhaps this departure is based upon a salary or benefits issue, in which case the managing partner may need to review whether the firm's scale is competitive. Perhaps problems with a supervisor exist, in which case the managing partner should examine the matter with the supervisor to determine whether working habits need to change.

Another issue that comes into play is whether or not the departure is expected. If an internal problem caused this departure, and comes as a surprise, why was the issue not raised earlier? An analysis of such situations might result in an improvement of the firm's mentoring system.

One way or another, an employee's departure should serve as a lesson to the firm. If nothing else is learned from the departing employee, the managing partner should at least wish the departing employee well.

The Lost Partner

While firms do not pay as much attention as they should to the loss of a case, client, and employee, they certainly do when they lose a partner.

The departure of a partner gives rise to a number of issues. With respect to client-control issues, the issue is an ethical one. It is the client's right to determine representation, and the client should be informed of this right. With respect to economic issues, such as compensation and control over unbilled time and accounts receivable, the firm's partnership agreement should very clearly define them.

At our firm, all unbilled time and accounts receivable remain with the firm, but the departing partner receives a percentage upon collection, which encourages that partner to help the firm obtain collection.

The departure of a partner may give rise to a series of additional issues, and the managing partner needs to be prepared to address them. Is the departure the result of a compensation issue, and if so, what lessons could be learned? If the firm is quite profitable, is the compensation among partners inequitable? Is the departing partner unhappy with the firm's philosophy or with a major policy? Is the departure the result of a personality issue? The managing partner needs to conduct a candid discussion with the departing partner, and then follow up with what may be a series of discussions with other partners. The loss of a partner is a serious matter, and if a firm does not learn something from it, history may repeat itself. If such history repeats itself a few times too often, the firm's viability may well be in jeopardy.

The managing partner may be entirely blameless for a particular loss. Yet even if personally blameless, the loss may well represent a shortcoming in the firm's performance—for which the managing partner is ultimately responsible.

Practice Pointers | **6**

A few management techniques that I employed during my tenure really served both my firm and me quite well. They might also be helpful to you.

Walking the Halls

Walking the halls a couple of times each day taught me a great deal about the work habits of various personnel and the overall working atmosphere. The halls should be walked as an interested coworker, and not a police officer. As a managing partner, I made it a point to stop along the way to speak with individual lawyers and staff members, to ask how they were doing. Obviously, you can't speak with everyone, but it is surprising how much you learn after only a couple of casual conversations. A staff member may be experiencing a personal problem to which the firm should be sensitive. Follow-up may be required on a workload issue. And on many occasions, I have learned of a business problem a client is having—a problem with respect to which another client might be of assistance, thereby creating a potential synergy, something both clients appreciate.

An Open Door Policy

As managing partner, I attempted to keep my door open—although obviously there were times when I really needed to avoid interruption—to encourage any and all staff and lawyers to speak to me individually. At the very least, a managing partner should have office hours on a regular basis so that everyone at the firm has an opportunity to talk. Once someone is in the office, the door should be closed so that any discussion can be conducted candidly and confidentially.

While a managing partner should be accessible, it is important that the managing partner not make judgments about a particular person's complaint without first hearing from the other side. It is also crucial that a managing partner not preempt someone else's jurisdiction.

In my tenure, many times someone would complain to me about another person before he or she had even discussed the issue with that person. I would usually suggest that the two people sit down to talk it out and then offer my services if they could not work it out. There are instances, however, when the issue is delicate or the political reality is that two people cannot talk it out, in which case the managing partner may have to arrange some shuttle diplomacy.

The Face-to-Face Meeting

Memos and e-mails are necessary when a managing partner communicates with the partners or entire firm. When the managing partner needs to communicate to one person, and especially when it does not involve a routine issue, the managing partner should conduct a meeting face-to-face, rather than with a memo or e-mail message. If a point needs to be made to an individual—whether it is to a partner, associate, or staff member—the managing partner should be able to look that person in the eye and make that point. This type of personal communication also gives the other person an opportunity to present his or her case if necessary. Most important, it allows the managing partner and the individual in question the opportunity to discuss how this issue could and should be handled differently the next time.

Client Accessibility

Although the managing partner cannot possibly meet all of a firm's clients, he or she should make an effort to meet major clients. The managing partner should also be accessible to any and all clients. On the rare occasion that a client has a complaint with a lawyer and wishes to speak with the managing partner, the client should have every right to do so. The managing partner should listen carefully to the client, but before reaching any conclusions he or she should review the matter with the lawyer in question. The client deserves a prompt response, and if the client is right, the managing partner must take immediate action to ensure that the situation is rectified.

Reading

There is no shortage of published materials on various aspects of law firm management. While there are a number of excellent publications on law firm management, the managing partner's reading habits should be extensive—from treatises on management, such as Thomas Peters and Robert H. Waterman's *In Search of Excellence* (Warner, 1998), to business and trade publications, to great works of fiction and nonfiction. Pat Conroy's *Lords of Discipline* (Bantam, 1986) has had the greatest influence on my professional conduct. This is a wonderful novel about the experiences of four military students, having little to do with law firm practice—except for the fact that it deals so well with the concept of honor.

Keeping Your Eyes and Ears Open

Much can be learned by comparing notes with your friends, colleagues, and opposing counsels in the surrounding legal community. Especially in this day and age, when firms are merging, breaking up, and acquiring and losing entire practice groups, it is important for a managing partner to know what is going on in the business and legal community. In many cities, managing partners have organized discussion groups, which meet on a monthly basis to discuss how to handle the various concerns confronting today's firms.

As a managing partner, you may learn of potential legal talent to be recruited for your firm, new marketing techniques being adopted by your competitors, and trends in the practice of law by keeping your eyes and ears open. You may also discover a problem in your own firm—otherwise unknown, but one that you should address.

Don't Let Problems Fester

Not every problem in a firm can be immediately attended to, but a firm can not indefinitely place problems on the back burner, in the hope that they will disappear. Some problems work themselves out, but most do not. A dispute between individuals within a firm should be dealt with fairly promptly, especially if the dispute is at the partnership level. A larger issue, such as the review of the compensation scale for paralegals, may require a considerable amount of time, but if put off, will only affect morale. And bad morale quickly balloons when unhappy staff members complain to otherwise satisfied employees.

The Black Notebook

Everyone has his or her own way of remaining organized, but one important tool has really worked for me: the black notebook. As a managing partner and a lawyer with a busy practice over the years, I could never have functioned without it.

In my black notebook, one page lists the initials of my secretary, the key administrators, every partner, the associates with whom I work, and general categories for other associates, counsels, and staff. A separate page is dedicated to each day of the current month, each of the ensuing months of the year, and the next year. At the beginning of each month, I enter items that need follow-up with others in the coming days, weeks, and months. During the course of my day, once I address something on my list, I might cross it out, but then make the requisite entry on a subsequent page if additional follow-up is necessary. At the end of the day, I review that day's page and see if I need to reenter any items I did not get to, and then look at the page for the next day. The notebook is convenient because it is something I can easily carry around and reminds me of items I may need to address as I am speaking with various personnel. It is also handy for jotting down new entries as matters come up when I am away from my desk or out of the office.

Qualities of the Managing Partner 7

The selection of a firm's managing partner should not be made by default or automatically awarded to a founding partner. Nor should the responsibility be thrust upon the partner who is least busy with client matters. The managing partner plays a critical role in defining the firm's goals and in establishing and carrying out policies and practices that allow the firm to achieve its goals. In selecting a managing partner, the firm's partnership should look for persons having the following eleven attributes.

Honesty and Integrity

It is an absolute given that the managing partner must possess great honesty and integrity. The managing partner is not simply entrusted with safeguarding the firm's finances but of commanding the trust of the entire firm and upholding the firm's reputation in the outside world.

Ability to Command Respect

One can be the most honest person in the world but have no ability to command respect from others. In law firms, it is necessary to command everyone's respect, including the most senior partners. Ideally, the managing partner must possess a good practice and solid legal skills; without such, the managing partner will carry less credibility with the more senior partners and experience difficulties when procuring their cooperation.

Good Instinct and Judgment

A firm may have the most rational and well-developed policies and practices, but not everything can be perfectly spelled out. A managing partner is required to interpret policies and determine when to make exceptions. A matter may simply not be covered by an existing policy. A managing partner needs good instincts and judgment to know when to enforce the rules, when to bend them, and when and how to fill the gaps. It is knowing when and how to be fair to the individual but also to the firm.

Leadership Skills

Leadership may be defined in many different ways, but ultimately, the proof is in the pudding. Is this leader someone who, by force of personality, can set an example and win the trust and respect of others so that they will follow his or her lead?

Political science scholar Richard Neustadt has defined the "power to persuade" as the most important element of presidential leadership. In *Presidential Power and the Modern Presidents* (Free Press, 1991), Neustadt writes that presidents are better served when they utilize persuasion as opposed to command.

The same argument may be made in the law firm setting. While a managing partner may have to resort to command, it is much more productive to employ the techniques of persuasion to move individuals and the overall firm toward a certain goal. The use of persuasion brings others into the process, making it far more likely for a meeting of minds.

Awareness and Perspective

The managing partner must be aware of what is going on in the firm. Walking the halls helps, as does feeling free enough to step into colleagues' offices to find out what is going on. Yet the managing partner must also have some perspective of the broader picture—of how a decision in one case affects the larger firm—both in the context of past practice and future implications.

The Ability to Make Decisions

During the course of any day, the managing partner may make a number of decisions, which range from the mundane to the critical and far-reaching. The managing partner must ensure that he or she is receiving the requisite input, considering the quality of the information and the various options. Once the requisite input is received, the managing partner should be decisive. Contemplation and reflection are obviously part of the process, but hemming and hawing should not be. Worse yet is avoidance. Unresolved issues tend to fester and only lead to demoralization.

Vision and Initiative

At most firms, partners are too busy with the demands of day-to-day practice to think about, let alone formulate and properly consider, a vision for the firm's future. The managing partner's must address those short-term and long-term issues that the firm should address.

Organizational Skills

A managing partner needs to be very well organized, especially if handling a significant practice on top of managing the firm. Someone can be both a great lawyer and manager, but if he or she is not well organized, failure will be encountered on both fronts.

Confidence and Self-Esteem

The managing partner should possess confidence. You cannot make effective decisions if you are not confident in what you are doing; you cannot serve as a good role model within the firm if you do not have confidence in yourself. You cannot represent the firm if you do not exude self-esteem.

An Understanding of What Hat to Wear

On some occasions the managing partner must be the master and take undisputed control over a situation; at other times, the managing partner acts as servant at the behest of the partnership or entire firm. The managing partner's most effective role is as peer. Knowing which hat to wear and when to wear it is important—and so is the ability to instantaneously change those hats.

A Sense of Humor

And finally, it helps to have a managing partner with a good sense of humor—someone who can keep things light and laugh at him or herself.

It is not every partner who embodies these eleven qualities. And those who do possess them may not have the desire to serve as managing partner. It is important that a firm's partners identify a qualified partner and persuade that person to take on this essential job.

PART II

Building the Infrastructure

Governance | **8**

When a partner assumes the managing partner position, the firm's governing structure will most likely be established and defined in the partnership agreement. Yet this governing structure may not be appropriate for the firm, and the managing partner should not accept it as a fait accompli. At the same time, however, the managing partner cannot be a despot, however beneficent, by simply doing away with or ignoring existing structures. The managing partner must work within the firm's processes to effectuate the needed structural and organizational changes.

The firm must also find the proper balance between the need for efficient and intelligent decision-making and the individual partner's desire to be heard. For a firm to operate successfully, numerous decisions need be made. Some decisions have far-reaching consequences; others relate to the day-to-day operation. Some partners wish to have a say in everything, while others wish to concentrate on the practice of law and to defer the rest to the managing partner.

The governing structure of a law firm should be partly determined by a firm's size and number of partners. What works well for a smaller firm may prove too unwieldy for a larger one. What proves effective for a larger firm may be undemocratic and unacceptable to a smaller one.

The Small Firm: Governance by Consensus

In very small firms—those consisting of fewer than ten partners—most of the key issues should be preserved for the partners, who should be operating by a consensus as opposed to simple majority vote. Obviously there will be differences of opinion on issues, and the majority should prevail. Yet when there are so few partners—who are no doubt working very closely with one another—it is difficult to preserve stability and morale if five partners consistently out-vote four of their colleagues on important issues. While the partnership agreement may call for majority vote, the managing partner of the smaller firm has an increased obligation to achieve consensus on important issues. This may mean spending more time preparing for partnership meetings by meeting privately with one or two partners at a time to forge common understandings. It may also mean spending additional time with individual partners in the wake of 5 to 4 votes to ensure that resentment is kept to a minimum.

The Midsized Firm: Partnership Democracy

In firms with ten to approximately twenty partners, consensus decision-making is desirable, but most partners understand that this cannot always be achieved. The managing partner should be entrusted with the authority to make many decisions, but larger issues should be reserved for the partners, who should operate as a democracy. The managing partner needs to ensure that partners are receiving reliable and sufficient information and that the pros and cons of various options are being presented. The managing partner, presumably acting as the chair of the partnership meetings, also needs to make sure that the differing viewpoints of partners are being presented.

In this type of model, the firm and its managing partner should consider whether certain votes require super-majorities. For example, it is hard to conceive of a healthy situation in which ten partners are out-voting nine over the admission of a new partner. This situation requires a super-majority vote, perhaps as high as 80 percent. If the partnership agreement does not already define the issue, the managing partner should review and propose an amendment that calls for super-majority votes on such issues as admitting new partners, relocations, and mergers.

The Larger Firm: The Need for a Management Committee

When the number of partners exceeds twenty, a firm needs to consider the advisability of a management or executive committee. The partners would still meet regularly but with fewer decisions reserved for partnership consideration. In the absence of a management committee, too many issues may be reserved to the partnership, and intelligent decision-making suffers. If there is a full airing on every item, partnership meetings will become unduly prolonged, and future attendance will suffer. If debate is curtailed so that the meetings are of reasonable duration, however, an insufficient airing of views may mean that the partnership does not make the right decision.

A management committee can perform two important functions for the larger firm. First, it can more efficiently and effectively decide on numerous issues, thereby allowing the partnership agenda to concentrate on major concerns. Second, the management committee can fully review the various options relevant to major issues and make recommendations, which would help facilitate partnership consideration.

It is critical to create a structure for the management committee that properly defines its scope of authority and is fair when it comes to the election of its members. Partners will not be happy if the management committee is delegated excessive authority. They will be equally unhappy if the membership of the management committee remains the same year after year. Term limits and rotations can address these concerns.

Bringing About Change

As firms grow, they need to review whether their existing governing structures are working effectively. There may be tension between those partners of longer standing—who dominate firm governance and may be resistant to change—and newer partners—who may believe that they have little influence on the partnership's decision-making and may have less respect for historical precedent. In this situation, the managing partner may need to convene representatives of different age and practice groups to review the firm's decision-making apparatus.

Regardless of the form of governance, once an important decision is made, all the partners should understand the rationale for that decision. The firm should establish a confidential vehicle within the partnership for addressing dissenting views. There should be no tolerance for partners grousing about decisions to non-partners.

A law firm cannot succeed unless it has a governing structure that promotes good decision-making and that is accepted by the partners of the firm. The managing partner needs to assess whether effective decision-making is being promoted and whether there is partnership acceptance of the governance structure. If the answer to either of these questions is less than satisfactory, the managing partner must then work within the existing governing system of the firm to bring about change.

Working with Committees | 9

Committees are a necessary evil; law firms cannot function without them. The managing partner cannot do everything, and the partnership as a whole should not do it all. Committees can assist the managing partner and the partners by addressing specific concerns or handling particular management tasks.

The Potential Pitfalls

Just because it may be more efficient to have a committee handle a particular matter does not mean that the committee will make the right decision. The committee may fail because it did not do the requisite legwork, very possibly because committee members are busy lawyers who do not give sufficient priority to their administrative assignments. Or the committee may be dominated by a partner whose opinions are inconsistent with the firm's best interests.

Another potential risk is what Dr. Jerry Harvey identifies in *The Abilene Paradox* (Lexington, 1988). Harvey describes a July Sunday in the early 1960s in Coleman, Texas. Harvey, his wife, and his in-laws try to survive the 104-degree weather by playing dominoes and drinking lemonade in front of a fan. At one point, his father-in-law suggests that they take a drive to Abilene, 53 miles away, to have dinner at a local cafeteria. Harvey thinks this is a terrible idea, especially since the trip to Abilene would be in an unair-conditioned 1958 Buick. But his wife chimes in, "Sounds like a great idea. How about you, Jerry?" Harvey meekly responds that it is fine by him, assuming that his mother-in-law is agreeable. She, in turn, does not want to be the dissenting vote so agrees to the drive. Off they go.

Four hours and 106 miles later, after two excruciatingly long, hot, and dusty drives, and a very mediocre meal, the four return home in silence. In an attempt to break the silence, Harvey says, in a tactful but less-than-honest way, "That was a great trip, wasn't it?" After a few moments of silence, one by one, each family member complains that it was a terrible idea and that he or she really wanted to stay home. Even Harvey's father-in-law admits that he had only raised the idea because he thought the others were bored. Harvey uses this anecdote to explain how organizations often go in the wrong direction because of bad decision-making processes.

In the context of a committee, the Abilene Paradox appears when one committee member articulates a proposal that makes no sense. Yet no one else wants to be so impolitic as to speak up and challenge it. Law firms are especially prone to the Abilene Paradox because undue deference is all too often paid to major rainmakers. Rainmakers may be talented at making rain, but that doesn't always mean that they have the best judgment when it comes to management issues.

At the other extreme, a committee may listen to too many people, and in an effort to make sure that no one is offended, comes up with a solution that is based upon a conglomeration of five different viewpoints. In short, the committee that was asked to produce a horse builds a camel.

Avoiding the Pitfalls

The managing partner can and should play a very significant role in the proper functioning of the firm's committees. He or she should review the overall committee structure, appoint the committee and its chair, define the scope of the committee's work, monitor the committee's deliberations and work, and work with the committee to finalize reports.

In the first instance, the managing partner should review the overall structure of the firm's committees. The firm may have standing committees, such as a finance, computer, and hiring committee, but the managing partner may consider creating additional long-standing or temporary committees. Should a house committee be created to promulgate policies for the use and treatment of the firm's space and facilities? Is there a need for a library committee, or is the librarian capable of doing the job without committee input?

The managing partner should also consider whether there is a need to create ad hoc committees to consider particular concerns such as the firm's merit bonus policy or retirement plan.

The selection and size of a committee is crucial. Lawyers are busy, and there is no need to overly staff a committee. At the same time, the managing partner should ensure that the committee members are representative of the firm's different interests. It must also be made clear that those selected will do the requisite work.

Of crucial importance is the selection of the committee chair, who is likely to have the greatest influence on the committee's ultimate decisions. The chair is responsible for making sure that the committee is convening on a regular basis and properly performing its tasks. The major rainmaker should not be the committee chair if that person does not possess good judgment. If the political reality is that a rainmaker must be the chair, there should be members of the committee who have the backbone to challenge his or her opinions.

Once the committee is appointed, the managing partner should sit down with the entire committee—or at least the chair—to properly define the committee's tasks and the scope of the committee's work. Committee members should be clear on the time schedule within which the work is to be performed and the individual time commitments that will be expected from each of them. The committee should also understand how its work ties into the overall goals and functioning of the firm.

The managing partner should also monitor the committee's deliberations without threatening its autonomy. Committee work takes time, and generally that time is uncompensated. Those who commit to the committee do so with the expectation that they will have some autonomy in addressing important firm concerns.

The managing partner should be an ex officio member of all committees in the firm, having the right to attend sessions and provide input. If the managing partner is overly involved, however, the committee members may feel suffocated, and the committee's purpose is defeated. Yet the other extreme can be equally unfortunate. If the managing partner is not paying attention and the committee goes so far afield that its work is not accepted by the partners, disappointment and frustration sets in. In short, the managing partner must find the appropriate balance in monitoring the committee's work.

The managing partner should have a good sense of how the partnership will react to a committee's report. The managing partner should work with the committee chair to finalize the report so that the requisite information and options are presented and recommendations are well-founded and properly supported.

If the subsequent partnership deliberation disapproves of the committee report, the managing partner needs to determine whether the report should be returned to the committee. A recommendation can often be reworked to meet partnership acceptance. If it is clear that the committee is unable to come up with any reformulation acceptable to a majority of the partners, remand to the committee should be avoided—it will only result in lost time and frustration.

The managing partner needs committees to assist in the proper functioning of the firm because he or she cannot handle it all alone. Yet the managing partner must take the time to monitor the committees to ensure that they are indeed contributing to the effective management of the firm.

Departments and Practice Groups | 10

If a firm's governing structure and committees define its political map, its departmental structure and practice groups determine the firm's natural resource map. Just as the managing partner must function effectively with the firm's governing structure and committees, so, too, must the managing partner function well with the firm's departments and practice groups. The managing partner needs to make sure that the firm is properly organized in practice groups, that the practice groups are performing their tasks, and that there is coordination among those practice groups.

Defining the Practice Groups

The threshold issue for the managing partner is whether the firm is properly organized in departments and practice groups. The law is simply too complex for individual lawyers to do everything. One of the advantages a firm has over a solo practitioner is that its lawyers can specialize, which increases their expertise and better serves the firm's clients. Most firms are organized into departments and practice groups, which allow lawyers within given specialties to work with one another. The managing partner should take the time to review the overall organization of the firm's departments and practice groups.

A firm's departments might be defined too broadly. When we were very small, our firm formed a business department, consisting of lawyers practicing in the areas of corporate, tax, real estate, and trusts and estates. As the law became more complex, however, it became obvious to me, as managing partner, that it was impossible for our business department lawyers to be at the cutting edge of each of these specialties. We needed to have narrower departments, with lawyers focusing on one or two of those four areas of law. This required a fair amount of partnership discussion, but we ultimately agreed to reorganize into separate departments, which has worked out very well for us.

Monitoring Practice Group Meetings

Departments and practice groups should meet regularly for a variety of purposes: to review new developments in the law, discuss client representations, monitor continuing legal education and training issues, discuss standards of practice, coordinate marketing efforts, and monitor workloads. The managing partner should regularly consult with department chairs to confirm that meetings are conducted on a regular basis, properly attended, and dealing with important issues. If the hours of lawyers within the department are below standard, the managing partner should consult with the relevant chair. And when departmental hours are higher than usual, the managing partner should initiate a discussion on the potential need to recruit additional lawyers. The managing partner should also consult with a department chair if concerns arise over a particular lawyer's quality of work in the department.

Coordination Between and Among Practice Groups

The managing partner should initiate a system to promote proper communication and cooperation between departments.

1. *The managing partner should take steps to ensure that every lawyer fully understands the expertise and capabilities offered by all departments in the firm.* Lawyers all too often have tunnel vision, focusing on the particular issues of law presented by their clients rather than the potential needs of clients outside their particular expertise. Lawyers need to be aware of the specialties of other departments so that they can be better attuned to how the firm can service their clients' needs.

2. *The managing partner should create a clear process for work referrals across departmental lines.* For example, if a trial department lawyer brings in an estate planning matter and delegates the work to a trust and estates associate, he or she should not expect to supervise that work. A system should be in place to ensure that the assignment is coordinated with the department chair or a partner within the trusts and estates department so that the work is properly supervised.

3. *The managing partner should be prepared to negotiate and adjudicate interdepartmental disputes.* For example, an associate might be a member of both the trial department and the employment law practice group. If there are competing demands upon that associate's time from the two departments, the managing partner may be required to mediate a solution, perhaps by having trial department assignments to the associate limited to employment litigation and then finding alternative resources for the trial department.

Perhaps the most important function of the managing partner's coordination of departments and practice groups is to remind everyone that they are working for the firm, not a particular department. All too often, department members think that their particular department is the most important in the firm, or that their department is supporting another one. Even if the corporate department is originating all of the work of the trial department—and this would rarely be the case at any firm—the lawyers in the corporate department must realize that they need the trial department lawyers as much as the trial department lawyers need them. The managing partner needs to play a role in helping these lawyers understand the bigger picture.

Rules and Policies **11**

If the partnership agreement is the constitution of a law firm, then the rules and policies are its statutes, and the way they are enforced is the firm's common law. The managing partner plays an integral role in ensuring that the firm's rules and policies have a solid foundation and that their implementation and enforcement are rational and intelligent.

Initial Review of the Firm's Rules and Policies

The managing partner should review the various rules and policies of the firm in light of the following considerations:

1. *What is the rationale for the rule?* All rules and policies should exist to promote a larger goal of the firm, be it quality service to clients or promoting a healthy working atmosphere. If there is no adequate rationale for the rule, it should not exist (especially because it is likely not to be respected and followed).

2. *Is the rule plainly stated and intelligible?* All rules and policies should be written in plain and simple terms rather than legalese. Rules cannot be followed unless they are easily understood and intelligible.

3. *Does everyone at the firm know about this rule?* Staff, lawyers, partners, and particularly new personnel should be familiar with all the rules and policies of a firm. The managing partner should create a central repository for the various rules and policies, such as in the staff handbook.

4. *Is the rule being followed?* In his novel, *The Cider House Rules* (Ballantine, 1994), author John Irving addresses rules that should be broken. Irving writes of the illogic of the rules posted at the cider house—although this is simply microcosmic for Irving's critique of laws restricting abortion. Law firms cannot afford to have rules that are honored in the breach. If a rule is not being followed, the firm should change the rule or enforce it better.

5. *Is the managing partner prepared to enforce the rule and address violations?* The rule becomes meaningless unless it is enforced. If the managing partner does not feel that he or she can enforce a rule or address violations, the rule needs to be reviewed.

The managing partner should consider the overall breadth and number of rules and policies. Law firm personnel, be they partners, associates, or staff, do not like to be overwhelmed or suffocated by excessive rules and policies. The managing partner might discover, for example, that the rules are important but that the number and wording of rules can be dramatically simplified.

On the other hand, the managing partner may discover voids in the firm's policies. The number and types of policies will vary from firm to firm, but every firm should have the following five rules and policies.

◆ *An expertise policy*, which provides that any work in a given area of law should be performed or supervised by a lawyer with expertise in that area.

◆ *Rules regarding standards of practice*, which addresses such issues as continuing legal education, returning of phone calls, and the format of letters and legal documents.

◆ *A confidentiality policy*, which calls for the preservation of any and all client confidences outside the firm.

◆ *A policy regarding the receipt of funds*, which includes compliance with all ethical requirements regarding clients' funds.

◆ *A policy prohibiting sexual harassment, as well as any harassment or discrimination* on the basis or gender, race, national origin, sexual preference, or disability.

It is essential that a firm address these five areas, yet firms will need additional rules and policies as well. The managing partner should consider whether existing policies address the firm's major problems. For example, a firm may have trouble collecting receivables but no established policy for dealing with aging receivables. A firm may have issues with how certain lawyers treat staff, but no code of conduct for interpersonal behavior. The managing partner must take the lead in determining whether new policies need to be promulgated.

When new policies are put into action, the managing partner should make sure that they have partnership backing. The managing partner should appear at meetings of staff and associates (assuming the policy applies beyond the partners) to present the policy and its rationale.

Enforcing the Rules

The managing partner must exercise care and skill when enforcing the rules since he or she must often address exceptions to those rules, both before and after the fact. There is a fine line between bending and breaking rules, and some rules cannot be bent at all. It is a matter of the managing partner's judgment and perspective.

This judgment and perspective is also needed when determining a penalty for a violation. It is difficult to write rules that definitively provide penalties if a rule is violated. Because various types of violations of one rule may exist, it may be imprudent to define up front what the penalty will be. The issue is often left to the managing partner's discretion. In exercising that judgment, the managing partner must also be prepared to recognize the importance of consistency. Inconsistent penalties will lead to resentment and dissatisfaction, especially if others perceive that the managing partner is favoring partners over others. The managing partner should recognize the need for perspective: a *de minimus* violation should merit a lesser penalty than an egregious one.

A firm's rules and policies and how they are enforced will play a significant role in defining the firm's overall culture and morale. Thus, the managing partner must take great care in addressing this area.

Information Technology | 12

Information technology touches upon virtually every aspect of the legal practice. Indeed, a firm's computer and electronic systems constitute its central nervous system. Although the managing partner need not be a computer wizard or Internet expert, he or she must be attuned to the many issues arising from the increased importance of information technology to the practice of law.

To ensure that a firm is making optimum use of information technology, the managing partner must establish a system that facilitates communication between lawyers and information technology (IT) personnel. Even if lawyers do not become fully computer proficient, IT personnel must educate lawyers on what tools and resources are available to them. And to learn how they can properly address lawyers' needs, IT personnel must interact with lawyers.

The need for a computer committee is essential. The computer committee at our firm is chaired by a computer literate partner, and includes our top two IT personnel and representatives of key practice groups. We make sure that the membership also includes at least one associate, one paralegal, and one secretary. These individuals represent those staff members who will work most closely with our computer systems, and it is essential that we receive their input and feedback.

The managing partner should be a regular member of this computer committee and should communicate to the committee selected elements of the firm's strategic plan. This discussion will no doubt elicit thoughts from committee members on how advances in its information technology will promote the firm's goals and objectives. The managing partner must also actively participate so that he or she can fully understand any available options. The newest, biggest, and brightest system may not necessarily be the best for the firm. Even if it is, the new system may not be a sufficient enough advance over existing systems to justify the money and time required to purchase it and train personnel.

The managing partner, with the assistance of a computer committee, should address the following eight concerns.

Resources

Computerization and the Internet offer a myriad of potential resources to law firms:

- Time and billing systems.
- Conflicts checks.
- Word processing.
- Legal research.
- Docketing and scheduling.
- Document management.
- Form files.
- Electronic filing.
- Electronic communications.
- Remote access.

In addition, the Internet, which has been described as having as profound an impact as the invention of the Gutenberg printing press in 1456, offers firms numerous tools and information. Lawyers can readily and efficiently access a wealth of data that in the past was either inaccessible or too expensive.

The managing partner must understand what resources are available to maximize the firm's effective and efficient delivery of legal services to clients. The managing partner must also be aware of how the competition is utilizing information technology.

Training

A firm may have state-of-the-art computer systems, but if its personnel are not properly trained, then the systems are wasted. The managing partner must oversee personnel training programs that recognize that different personnel require different levels of training. The managing partner will discover that there are some lawyers, most likely senior partners, who are resistant to any type of training, and may simply refuse to use computers. The firm has every right, and indeed an obligation to its clients, to require that all lawyers, including the "dinosaurs," obtain a minimum level of proficiency, including communicating by e-mail and opening up, editing, and producing documents. For secretaries, paralegals, and lawyers who are quite computer literate, the firm should make available more sophisticated training to permit full advantage of the firm's systems.

Feedback

Hopefully the firm properly tests new systems before putting them in place. The most comprehensive testing cannot anticipate all issues, however, and it is important that the firm establish a method for obtaining feedback from users. Tweaking and adjustment may satisfy many concerns, but the firm must also be prepared to deal with more serious issues. If a mistake has been made, the firm must rectify the situation and learn from it.

Security

The managing partner must ensure that proper safeguards are implemented to protect the security of the firm's computer systems.

This is especially important given a lawyer's ethical obligation to preserve client confidences. Firms are utilizing systems that facilitate online interaction between lawyers and clients and that afford clients access to relevant file materials. While beneficial to both parties, these systems must have checks in place so clients cannot access confidential files of other clients or the firm.

Needless to say, a firm's computer systems must also be fully secured to prevent access to client files by outsiders. A firm must also establish a system of passwords and restricted access that guarantees that persons within the firm cannot access confidential firm files.

Although the IT personnel may be extremely confident about the security of the firm's computers, the managing partner should strongly consider retaining outside experts to conduct a security audit.

Usage Policy

With the assistance of the computer committee, the managing partner should put in effect a usage policy to address personal use and software installation. A policy that bans personal use altogether is unlikely to be followed or respected—just as it is not feasible to ban all personal phone calls. The more prudent and realistic course is to require that personal use be kept to a minimum and not interfere with a person's job.

On the subject of privacy, it must be made clear that any and all computer files are the property of the firm—and the firm has the right to examine any files. The computers belong to the firm, and it may be necessary—such as in the case of an investigation of misconduct—to access employee files. At the same time, it should be made clear to all that a Big Brother atmosphere is not being promoted. The managing partner should spread the message that, although the firm reserves the right to examine any computer files, in actual practice the firm will not do so, except on the very rare occasion of an investigation into misconduct.

A usage policy must also address the installation of new software. In addition to prohibiting the installation of any unlicensed software, the policy should stipulate that all software installations be coordinated through the director of information technology, who will conduct an anti-virus check. When conducting these crucial virus checks, the firm should not rely upon an outdated anti-virus program. Viruses are constantly being developed to attack certain computer programs, and it is essential that a firm owns the latest update of an anti-virus program.

Contingency Plans/Back-up

The managing partner must also ensure that the firm establishes a system to deal with contingencies. Mechanisms should be in place for an immediate response to a shutdown or other problems. Information technology personnel should be on call at all times and outside service providers should be engaged to respond quickly to technical difficulties. A contingency plan must also be established to deal with an electrical shutdown, fire, or other disaster. Systems should be constantly backed up, with back-up tapes stored in secured on-site and off-site locations.

Ethical Issues

The managing partner must be attuned to the ethical issues arising from computerization. For example, the Internet may provide access to an opposing party's Web page. Yet if a lawyer is accessing and communicating with that Web page, a violation of the disciplinary rule prohibiting communications with parties represented by counsel may occur.

Another ethical issue the firm and managing partner must address is how to charge for services that have become much more efficient with the use of computers. A sophisticated form file may now permit a lawyer to produce work in a highly efficient manner.

The inclination is to have the client pay for the value of the product. If the billing arrangement is on the traditional hourly basis, however, it is entirely unfair, and indeed unethical, to bill the client anything more than the hours worked. If hours are lower because of computer efficiencies, so be it. The lawyer may charge the client a set price representing the value of the form, but that should be worked out with the client at the outset.

Telecommuting

The computer age provides various opportunities for lawyers to work from home, and the managing partner should consider a telecommuting policy. Such a policy may help employees create a better balance between their professional and personal lives, and a firm may find that offering the policy enhances its recruitment capabilities and reduces employee turnover. A viable argument may be made that lawyers can work more productively from time to time if they are away from the daily interruptions at the office, and that the time saved on commuting can be used for more productive purposes.

The problem is that associates need to be accessible to partners, and an associate is less accessible if working from home. While a partner who is highly adept with computers can function fairly well from home, it does not serve the firm to allow partners significantly greater telecommuting rights than associates. Partners also need to be accessible to associates, which means being available in the office.

Advances in remote access provide the technological capability of promulgating a telecommuting policy. The task for the managing partner is to develop a policy that strikes a balance between the benefits of telecommuting with the need for partners and associates to be accessible to one another.

Some final words of advice: first of all, computers are consistently being upgraded. Rather than doing an entire upgrade at once, the firm might consider a rolling upgrade program, with higher-end users getting the first upgrade, and lower-end users obtaining it the next year. Such a system saves costs and allows the firm the opportunity to satisfy itself with the upgrade. The inevitable next upgrade also becomes easier to do.

Second, the overall process never ends. As long as advances continue to be made in information technology, which of course they will, a firm must be aware of and able to evaluate new options and improvements. The competition is doing the same thing, and a firm's clients deserve the most efficient and effective delivery of legal services.

PART III

Maximizing Human Resources

Treatment of Staff **13**

A law firm cannot survive without a good support staff. Staff should be treated with dignity and respect, and law firms that recognize these principles are much more likely to attract and retain a good and truly supportive staff.

Lawyers, and especially partners, may be difficult to work with. Many lawyers tend to be forceful and aggressive by nature and the demands of the legal practice can often exacerbate these personality traits. All too often, lawyers are solipsistic, believing that nothing else in the world exists or is anywhere near as important as their own practices.

The consequences for secretaries, paralegals, and other support staff members who work with such lawyers can be severe. Support staff members can be demeaned or blamed for less than perfect work. And perfect work may easily be taken for granted.

A firm's management must create a working atmosphere where the dignity and respect of support staff is promoted, and where support staff members are happy and productive. A firm can implement a number of policies and practices to advance this healthy working environment. The following policies and practices have proven effective for our firm over the years.

Code of Interpersonal Conduct

Several years ago, when it appeared that some of our firm's lawyers were not paying sufficient respect to the support staff, we devoted a portion of a partnership retreat to this important issue. As a result, the partnership, in consultation with associates and staff, formally adopted a Code of Interpersonal Conduct, which includes the following basic principles:

◆ Respect, dignity, and common courtesy are the common denominators for all personal conduct and communication at the firm.

◆ All personnel should make an effort to understand the job duties, responsibilities, and pressures of others.

◆ All personnel should engage in open and honest communication, and staff members should not be reluctant to speak up.

◆ Criticism is important to understanding how someone can improve his or her performance, but that criticism should be presented constructively and privately, with no one being publicly reprimanded or criticized.

◆ Gossip and rumors are contrary to the principles of respect and dignity.

◆ When someone puts in extra effort or does an exceptionally good job, the supervisor should communicate appreciation.

◆ It is often necessary to interrupt others, but interruptions should be made courteously and respectfully.

◆ There is no basis for assessing blame on someone who is not to blame.

These are simple and basic principles all too often forgotten by some lawyers. By formally adopting and promulgating a code, a firm can help promote long-term loyalty among staff.

Once a code is adopted, the firm must be prepared to deal with those, including partners, who fail to abide by it. In the instance of an individual deviation from the code, the matter needs to be brought to a lawyer's attention. This lawyer must recognize how the matter could have been handled differently. The lawyer might also owe that staff member an apology. In cases of repeat offenses, the firm must be prepared to sanction the lawyer, by way of fine or probation. And in situations of flagrant and ongoing disregard, the firm needs to be prepared to require a counseling program. If a lawyer refuses to participate in this counseling program, the firm should take steps to part ways with that lawyer.

Defining Responsibilities and Expectations

A staff member is entitled to a comprehensive description of his or her job responsibilities and the firm's expectations of his or her performance. This description may be communicated in the initial letter of employment or in the firm's staff manual. A job description offers a staff member a better understanding of his or her position and serves as a benchmark to review the staff member's performance. Regular feedback on individual assignments, consistent with the overall framework of job expectations, should be initiated. Annual employee reviews should be established, and the firm should treat these reviews as an important opportunity to engage employees in a productive dialogue on performance and expectations.

Team Building

A staff member's motivation is greatly enhanced when that employee is able to grasp the larger picture. All too often staff members are asked to handle discrete assignments, with no understanding of how their work ties in with the overall representation of the client. An individual word processing or research assignment becomes much more meaningful when a staff member realizes the role it plays in serving the client. It is human nature that we prefer to work on meaningful matters. This is certainly true for a lawyer, and is no less true for staff.

Ideally, the team—which may consist of a partner, associate, paralegal, and secretary—working on a given representation should meet on a regular basis to review the larger picture and how upcoming assignments tie into the overall goal. When this overall goal is accomplished for the client, each team member should, at the very least, be informed and should receive recognition for his or her contributions.

Encouraging People to Speak Up

It has been my experience over the years that the most valuable staff members are those who are not afraid to tell me what I should hear, rather than what they think I want to hear. Some of the best insights come from those who are closest to the situation. Unless staff members are encouraged to speak up, however, they may not, and the firm only suffers when a good idea or thought is not articulated.

The hierarchical nature of law firms can discourage staff members from offering their viewpoints. And partners who are pressured by client demands and billable hours are not generally receptive to dissenting opinions.

The managing partner must consistently get out the message that people should not be afraid to speak up. It is a given that there should be no negative repercussions for voicing one's views. To the contrary, when a staff member speaks up and suggests how something might be handled better, the feedback should be quite positive.

Keeping Things Light

The representation of client interests is a very serious undertaking, but this does not mean that a firm's working environment has to be serious and intense at all times. Because law firm personnel are under great pressure, it is essential to lighten things up from time to time.

At our firm, we endeavor to keep things light when possible. For example, we recognize birthdays and in addition to a summer outing and a holiday party, we have informal parties starting at 4:30 p.m. on the last Friday of each month. We host staff-only functions from time to time, such as a Chinese luncheon, an ice cream sundae get-together, or a wine-and-cheese party to view a late fall sunset. In December, we offer each staff member a half day off for holiday shopping. And after a full decade of playing my traditional April Fools' joke on the staff—with some on guard for it—I am happy to say that I was still fooling quite a few people. Basically, our firm tries to exhibit a sense of humor on a regular basis.

Attending to Personal Issues

Staff members do indeed have lives outside the office, and from time to time, a personal or family matter will interfere with an individual's job performance. The director of human resources can help the managing partner stay attuned to such issues.

A loyal and dedicated staff member should not be penalized if a personal or family issue is impeding that person's ability to follow firm rules and regulations. For example, when a secretary of long-term standing made a request to work 6 a.m. to 2 p.m. each day for a few months, so that she could attend to her terminally ill mother, our firm accommodated that request. And when a dedicated staff member needed to take a few weeks off for an operation, the firm was flexible in working with that person to ensure that it would not result in economic hardship.

When there is a death in a staff member's family, the managing partner and the firm should pay the appropriate respects. When a staff member has a personal problem that can be resolved by a call from one of the firm's partners, the call should be made.

When all is said and done, it simply comes down to a matter of human decency. A firm needs to be good to its staff members because they deserve to be treated decently. Ultimately, it is in the firm's best interests to exhibit decency to ensure long-term loyalty on the part of its staff.

Treatment of Associates 14

Virtually all law firms rely greatly on their associates, and it is disturbing that all too many firms fall short in their treatment of them. Associates are too often taken for granted. Whereas they should be viewed as important human resources, and potential building blocks for the firm's future growth, associates are viewed as easily replaced commodities.

An associate has a legitimate right to each of the following, and it is in the firm's interests to recognize these entitlements:

- ◆ A clear definition of the firm's policies and practices for promotion to partnership.
- ◆ Delegation of responsibilities correlating to the associate's experience and abilities.
- ◆ A mentor.
- ◆ Regular and ongoing supervision and training.
- ◆ A compensation package that recognizes the associate's contributions to the firm.
- ◆ Annual reviews, including an associate's right to know where he or she stands in terms of prospects for promotion.

◆ The firm's recognition that the associate has a right to a life outside the firm.

Definition of Policies and Practices Regarding Promotion

Firms are generally good about defining for associates what type of billable hours and quality of work is expected. A firm also owes associates a complete explanation of its policies and practices for promotion to partnership.

When it interviews and selects associates, a firm should consider not only the candidate's potential to be a good associate, but also the candidate's long-term potential for promotion to partnership. And the candidate should be considering not only what the experience at the firm will be as an associate, but also the longer-term picture.

It is certainly in the firm's best interests to disclose its expectations for promotion to partnership to a candidate—since the ideal hire is someone who will not only be a good associate but a productive partner. The firm benefits when these issues are defined up front, so that an associate fully understands what is expected and can work toward those goals. Disclosure of this type is also the fair thing to do since an associate is entitled to such information.

If developing a high proficiency level in a given area of law is a prerequisite to partnership, as it should be, the firm should explain how an associate can develop his or her proficiency and how the firm will assist in the development. And if building an established clientele is a prerequisite to partnership, the firm should develop a marketing program and mentoring system to help the associate build such a clientele.

The firm that does not have a clear track record and established standards for promotion to partnership should formulate such criterion and be prepared to live up to those standards. It will discover that a clear definition of partnership promotion expectations and a track record consistent with those expectations will help it attract and retain the best associates over the long run.

Delegation of Responsibilities

An associate is entitled to a delegation of those responsibilities that best correlate with his or her experience and abilities. As an associate gains additional experience and improves in ability, he or she should receive an increase in responsibilities. Otherwise, there cannot be any real growth.

Clearly it is in the firm's interests to ensure that its associates are receiving increased responsibilities. The firm's long-term growth is dependent upon the continued growth and improvement of associates and the promotion to partnership of deserving associates.

A Mentor

The firm should establish a mentoring system that assigns an individual mentor to each associate. This mentor should be a partner within the associate's practice group, should meet with the associate on a regular basis, and otherwise be available to discuss issues such as:

- ◆ Professional development issues.
- ◆ Workload issues.
- ◆ Problems with partners with whom the associate works.
- ◆ Complaints about the firm.
- ◆ Annual goals.

The managing partner should establish a system to ensure that mentors meet regularly with associates and keep the managing partner advised of important developments. The managing partner should not hesitate to change mentor assignments if the mentor is not doing his or her job or if the relationship between the mentor and associate is less than satisfactory.

Another benefit of a good mentoring system is that it can greatly reduce the rate of associate turnover because the firm becomes better attuned to issues affecting associate morale.

Supervision and Training

Even the brightest associates cannot grow if they do not receive the requisite supervision and training. This is where even the best of firms fall short.

Proper supervision and training of associates requires time— time that is not necessarily billable to the client—and patience on the part of the partners. It is all too easy for partners, caught up in the demands of clients and the firm, to devote an insufficient amount of time to reviewing assignments with associates.

Nevertheless, the firm owes it to its associates to review every assignment on an individual basis. And frankly the firm owes it to its clients to ensure that the associate's work is competently done. If the firm is shortchanging its associates, it also risks shortchanging its clients.

Fair Compensation

In most cities, larger firms are competing for the best and brightest of associates. As a result, they offer quite generous compensation packages. The experience at midsized and smaller firms is much more varied. Many such firms are guided by what the larger firms are offering, since they are operating in the same general marketplace. Certain firms set their own standards, indifferent to the overall marketplace, and some may be taking advantage of their associates, plain and simple.

For reasons of fairness and dignity alone, a firm should not be able to treat associates unjustly and unfairly. Respect for associates' overall contributions to the firm needs to exist. It is definitely in the firm's best interests to fairly compensate its associates. An undercompensated associate will start to resent the firm over the long term, and the firm will only jeopardize its retention of better associates.

Annual Reviews

Firms should conduct a formal review of their associates on an annual basis, if not more. The review, based upon feedback by partners who have worked with that associate, should address his or her performance over the past year, goals for the coming one, and where things stand in the long-term picture for partnership promotion. Ideally, the review should be a dialog between the reviewing partner(s) and associate.

This review should include a constructive critique of the associate's performance by the partners. The associate should also be permitted to constructively critique the firm and encouraged to offer suggestions on how his or her experience at the firm can be improved. Firms need to recognize that it is not easy for associates to air their views. Associates have to be encouraged to speak up because it is only through a healthy two-way dialogue that both parties can understand each other. Not every suggestion or critique by the associate will be accepted by the firm, and partners should not feel duty bound to accept every suggestion. Yet the associate is entitled to a fair explanation of why something is not a good idea. Assuming that this explanation is based upon some semblance of rationality and principle, the associate will have a greater appreciation and respect for the firm's position.

It is essential that the firm is honest and candid with an associate during a review, especially on the issue of partnership prospects. All too often, firms give associates good reviews year after year, only to tell that associate in year seven that he or she will not become a partner. This is unfair to the associate. An associate performing below expectations should be so informed at the earliest possible time. The associate should be told what is required to improve, and that associate should then be given an opportunity to improve. If sufficient improvement is not made, and it becomes clear that partnership is not a realistic prospect, the associate must be told.

It is much easier for an associate to move on to another firm after two or three years than it is after seven or eight. To string along an associate is unfair. And again, it is in the firm's best interest not to do so. If a firm wishes to attract and retain good associates over the long term, it must be fair to its present associates.

Recognition of Outside Life

It is all too easy for a firm to establish unreasonably high expectations for billable hours and to demand that its associates compete with one another in posting exorbitant hours. After all, the leveraging of associates can enhance partnership profitability.

Obviously client needs must be met, and if the midnight oil has to be burned to meet a deadline, then so be it. Yet associates are entitled to a personal life.

The question is one of degree and frequency. Individuals who choose to work in the legal profession, particularly at private firms, understand that from time to time they need to make sacrifices to properly serve their clients. If associates are constantly burning the midnight oil and working exorbitant hours, however, the firm needs to hire more associates—the firm can afford it.

Lawyers are recognizing the importance of prioritizing their lives, to not unduly sacrificing personal and family commitments to the demands of practice. Firms that are able to meet the needs of these lawyers will find that they are in a better position in the marketplace to attract and retain good people.

Treatment of Partners | 15

It is a given that no two partners make identical contributions to a firm. And it is a given that no two partners of a firm have identical personalities. The greater the number of persons in the partnership, the greater the number of ways in which they will contribute, and the greater the types of personalities involved.

Perhaps the most challenging aspect of law firm management is to find an appropriate balance between the firm's need for structure and the partner's need to be treated individually. If the structure of the firm is too rigid, partners will not be sufficiently motivated to fully contribute. On the other hand, if partners are given too much autonomy, no one will know what the rules are, and disputes will inevitably arise.

Several key issues are involved in the treatment of partners. The common denominator is that each issue involves a balance between the needs of individual partners and the interests of the firm.

Compensation

Just as goals for individual partners must recognize their different contributions to the firm, so, too, must the partnership's compensation system. Again invoking a basketball analogy: scoring may be more valuable than rebounding; the player who both scores and plays defense is contributing more than the player who can just score. A law firm must establish individual goals for its partners, but if it wishes to properly motivate them, it cannot pay them all equally, or in some lockstep manner. Whether by way of formula or compensation committee, the different types of contributions made by individual partners must be differentially recognized.

What is important is that there be an overall rationality of the system, and a partnership consensus therefor. Many a firm has broken up over compensation issues. These break-ups typically result from a failure to achieve consensus ahead of time or a failure to anticipate unique situations.

Allow me to describe in very summary terms the formula we use in dividing partnership profits at our firm, a formula that has provided the right incentives and has contributed to our growth. Our profit is divided into four overall pools: production, delegation, turnover, and seniority.

Production, the largest pool, accounts for almost 60 percent of our overall profit and is defined as dollars collected for the partner's own time charges. In other words, we encourage our partners to work hard and to collect on their time. We use the numbers from the past three years to avoid the peaks and valleys of any given year, but we give greater weight to the present year. The partner receives a fraction of the production pool, where the numerator is his or her production during the current year and the two previous ones, and the denominator is the total production of all partners over the three-year period. We do not distinguish, for purposes of this pool, fees received from one's own clients versus fees received for one's time on other clients, because we do not want partners to favor their own clients over other clients of the firm.

The second largest pool is delegation, which accounts for about 30 percent of profit and consists of all time charges billed and collected by the billing partner, other than his or her own time charges. The pool is intended to reward those who bring clients into the firm and retain good relations with those clients. The mechanics are similar to the production pool, with the use of a three-year average and the analogous fraction.

The turnover pool, consisting of about five percent of profit, rewards those partners who turn over clients and relinquish billing lawyer status to other lawyers. The intent is to encourage our more senior lawyers to help build the practices of our younger ones. We make computations based upon the fees collected for the clients turned over, and divide the pool accordingly.

The fourth and final pool is the seniority pool, consisting of about five percent of profit. An associate promoted to partner receives three seniority points. Each year after that, the partner receives one additional point, until year eighteen. At that time, we give one-half point for each additional year. Our theory is that every year the partners are working to improve the overall firm, and that new partners are benefiting from the contributions made to date by the preexisting partners.

Our formula encourages partners to work hard, to delegate work, to turn over clients, and to collect their bills. Seniority plays a role, but at our firm one does not become wealthy by simply growing old. We have, in fact, reduced the percentage allotted to the seniority pool on several occasions over the years. The formula is up for amendment every three years but not before then, unless there is an 80 percent vote. That way everyone knows what the rules are, and understands that the rules cannot be changed too easily, has proven to be important to the overall stability of our firm.

The one element that we do not include in our formula, and arguably should, is some discretionary factor to reward administrative contributions and the training of associates. We actually established a small discretionary pool in our formula a number of years ago to encourage partners to do these things but eliminated it when we found we were spending too much time and energy on how to divide five percent of the pie. We simply expect that all of our partners will contribute to firm administration and the training of associates in one way or another.

Acceptance of Representations/Contingent Fee Cases

Partners desire autonomy when it comes to accepting particular cases and working in certain practice areas. At the same time, the firm needs to enforce rules in these same areas. The firm is not prepared to take on every client. A balance must be found.

It is important for a firm's partners to agree on the types of clients they will and will not take on and issues such as retainers and fee arrangements. It is particularly crucial to establish a policy for the acceptance of contingent fee cases. Firms need to review proposed contingent fee cases on an individual basis in the context of defined parameters. At our firm, a partner introducing a proposed contingent fee client must provide a written analysis that sets forth the likely amount of recovery—in light of the probability of demonstrating liability—and the value of the projected time charges. We typically do not accept a case that does not project an ultimate recovery—computed on a present value basis—in excess of our projected time charges. Firms also should consider the need for an appropriate balance between contingent fee work and traditional hourly work.

Personal Conduct

Partners have different personalities, but they do not practice in a vacuum. It is important for partners to feel that they are individuals yet their individuality should not interfere with the firm's overall operation.

Too often, some partners tend to believe that the entire firm (or world) revolves around them. Such partners can destroy an otherwise good firm. The individuality of partners must be encouraged, but partners must also be reminded that they are also part of the entire firm.

Addressing issues of personal conduct must be done in a delicate manner. Whereas the partners as a whole can address the division of firm profits, the acceptance of clients, and issues of firm governance, the entire partnership should not deal with questions of personal excess. The managing partner must take on the responsibility of addressing personal issues with the partner in question in a confidential manner.

The managing partner cannot be reticent, even when the partner who is engaged in questionable conduct is a major rainmaker.

When there is excessive or abusive conduct, the partner's rainmaking ability should be irrelevant. The entire firm may be held responsible for a partner's abuses, such as sexual harassment or unethical billing practices. The managing partner cannot be an ostrich in this matter. The situation must be immediately addressed.

Ideally, the managing partner should resolve the matter with the abusing partner in private. He or she must explain why such conduct is unacceptable and puts the interests of the entire firm at stake. A counseling arrangement might be established. If the abuse continues, the managing partner may no longer be in a position to keep the matter confidential, and is obligated to bring it to the attention of a small group of additional partners. This group of partners, under the direction of the managing partner, might confront the abusive partner. They should make it clear that they are prepared to present the issue to the partnership as a whole and to vote out the partner in question unless the abusive behavior ceases.

Ultimately the managing partner must make all the partners understand that the firm is bigger and more important than any one of them. The firm's overall viability and reputation leave no room for abusive or excessive behavior.

Accounts Receivable

Law firm partners make lousy bankers. When a partner allows a client to become too far extended in its bills, this partner is effectively asking the firm to loan money to the client so that it may pay its other bills. Rest assured that the client is meeting its payroll, paying its electric and rent bill, and probably most of its other creditors. The practical reality that the partner is lending the firm's money to the client is exacerbated by the ethical rules that restrict a firm's ability to charge interest.

Partners need to realize that accounts receivable are assets of the firm, not individual partners. Once this is accepted, the next thing they need to realize is that the partner may be the worst person to collect the receivable. A partner's personal relationship with his or her client may get in the way of pressing for payment. A partner may also simply be too busy to attend to collections.

Firms need to take control of receivables at ninety days—some would argue at sixty—and place the responsibility for collection in the hands of their accounting departments. The accounting staff member should discuss particular issues relevant to the client's non-payment with the partner, but that partner should not control the actions of the accounting department. If there is a dispute, the managing partner needs to step in.

A firm must also create procedures for terminating client relations when the receivable issue cannot be satisfactorily resolved. Obviously ethical procedures must be adhered to, particularly when a lawyer is representing a client on a litigation matter—leave of court will have to be obtained unless successor counsel is found. The client should receive sufficient notice of any termination and its interests must not be prejudiced by such action.

Stock for Services

Stock for services is an important issue for partners, especially in the era of e-commerce. At times a stock-for-service arrangement is a necessity, as a start-up enterprise may simply not have the financial wherewithal to retain counsel. Increasingly, however, firms are taking stock for services to obtain a share of the wealth.

A client has the right to independent legal counsel, and a lawyer has the concomitant ethical obligation to provide independent legal counsel. Stock-for-service arrangements may undermine a lawyer's ability to provide independent counsel if that lawyer's stake in the company is too great, either from a percentage or a straight monetary standpoint. The managing partner must remind partners of these ethical strictures.

In addition, stock-for-service arrangements raise other issues for a firm:

- *Who owns the stock? The firm, the originating partner, or the partners who work on the matter?*
- *If the firm owns the stock, what is the trigger for selling that stock?*

◆ *If a partner learns of a potential investment opportunity from a client, does the doctrine of corporate opportunity require that the firm and/or its partners be offered that opportunity?*

A managing partner should be sensitive to all these issues. If at all possible, a policy should be defined up front, before the issue is presented and the real money becomes an issue. In general, I would suggest that the following principles be applied:

◆ It is the firm that is rendering the services, and therefore, the firm should hold most of the stock. Yet the originating partner and the lawyers working on the matter are entitled to payment. If the firm cannot pay them in the usual way for their work, and if ultimate payment is entirely speculative, then a share of the stock, but certainly not all of it, should go to them.

◆ The firm should have the earliest possible trigger date for selling the stock, and a majority of partners should be able to pull the trigger.

◆ A partner has an obligation to disclose an investment opportunity presented by the client to the firm and its partners.

Each of these principles involves creating a balance between the autonomy of the individual partner and the proper functioning of the firm. The managing partner represents the firm, but the managing partner must recognize that individual partners are also very important to the firm.

Partnership Retreats

Sometimes it is helpful to have everyone step back from the day-to-day demands of practice. Partnership retreats can serve as an opportunity to address the balance between the firm and its individual partners. A retreat may also be an excellent opportunity for partners to consider a proposed long-term plan, a potential merger, or a major commitment to a new practice area.

Retreats should be conducted away from the office at off-hours. This new setting allows partners to consider an issue from a fresh perspective without interruption. The managing partner, perhaps assisted by a committee, should prepare the agenda ahead of time, and there should be partnership consensus on the issues to be discussed. The managing partner should also accumulate and compile the various materials to be reviewed by partners in advance.

Although it is commonplace for firms to retain outside facilitators to lead retreat discussions, I have chosen not to do so—primarily because of the confidential nature of the issues typically discussed. To ensure that the managing partner is not dominating the retreat proceedings, however, we have different partners chair different segments of the overall session.

The most important part of a retreat is the follow-up agenda. Some of the most wonderful and grandiose ideas may be discussed during the course of the retreat, but if there is not appropriate follow-up, all is for naught. The managing partner needs to take the lead in translating any good ideas into practice.

Special Situations | **16**

All firms must address special situations from time to time. The manner in which they address such situations is critical not only to the lawyers in question, but as an example to the rest of the firm. A firm that acts with sensitivity and understanding is more likely to successfully address a particular, individual case—and more likely to win the respect of its lawyers and support staff.

A firm should be prepared to face the following four types of special situations.

The Under-Productive Lawyer

There are many reasons why a lawyer may not be productive for a firm. Because there is no single explanation for a lack of productivity, there is no single solution. Each situation must be assessed on an individual basis, and only then can an appropriate solution to the problem be formulated.

In some cases, the under-productive lawyer is fully competent, with no shortage of work, but does not make the effort expected by the firm. In such cases, it is important for the managing partner and/or department chair to consult with the lawyer on a confidential basis. If there are personal or family issues interfering with the lawyer's efforts, the firm should show some understanding and offer its help. If, on the other hand, it is simply a matter of work ethic, the lawyer must be made to understand that he or she is hurting the firm by not contributing his or her due share and is setting the wrong example to others. The firm should establish a compensation formula that rewards a good work ethic so as not to cause resentment on the part of harder working partners.

Lack of production may also be explained by an absence of available work. The lawyer in question may be fully competent and have a very commendable work ethic, but there is simply not sufficient work to fill his or her plate. Obviously there should be a healthy discussion with the lawyer about potential marketing efforts. If marketing cannot provide a quick fix, the firm must determine how the lawyer might otherwise contribute. The firm should understand the potential demoralization of this lawyer and might consider giving the lawyer additional management assignments. The firm might also suggest that this lawyer take on pro bono assignments. Writing an article for publication, which helps to increase the exposure of the lawyer and the firm, might also be encouraged.

The most difficult situation to deal with is the lawyer whose underproduction is due to a lack of competence. The firm has a duty to its clients to ensure that competent practitioners are handling their matters. The firm cannot in good faith assign additional work to a less-than-competent lawyer, unless it is fully prepared to have a competent lawyer supervise the matter and discount this client's bill.

To address the situation of the under-productive, less than competent lawyer, the firm must be prepared to evaluate whether this lawyer is capable of competent practice, either through additional training and experience or retooling in another specialty. If this lawyer has the potential, the firm should devote sufficient resources and time to permit his or her development. It is certainly in the firm's best interests to work with this type of lawyer. If a lawyer simply does not have the tools to become competent, and there is no alternative way in which this lawyer can make a real contribution, the firm may have to part ways with this lawyer after allowing the lawyer sufficient time to find alternative employment.

The Lawyer Engaged in Substance Abuse

Substance abuse must be dealt with in a manner that is respectful of both the principles of the firm and the dignity of the individual. On the one hand, the firm has fiduciary responsibilities to its clients and expectations for its lawyers and staff. The substance abuse by one individual can threaten the firm's ability to serve its clients and demand acceptable performance from the remainder of its lawyers and staff. On the other hand, the firm must view substance abuse as a disease, something that is now beyond the control of the abuser. And just as a firm should mercifully treat a lawyer suffering from cancer, so, too, should mercy be exhibited toward a substance abuser.

Respecting both the principles of the firm and the dignity of the individual requires a program that is both tough and fair. Such a program should consist of the following seven steps.

1. *Consulting with a professional organization.* In Massachusetts, the organization Lawyers Concerned About Lawyers offers experienced and sound assistance in dealing with substance abuse. Many states have similar organizations.
2. *Confronting the abusing lawyer, in consultation with the professional, in a discreet manner.* The lawyer is informed that the firm is aware of the problem and is told what he or she will be required to do to remain with the firm.
3. *Requiring the abusing lawyer to enroll in a treatment program.* In consultation with a professional, the firm must find an appropriate program for the treatment of the abusing lawyer's problem, and the lawyer must be required to enroll in and complete the program. The progress of the lawyer should be monitored by the firm, but in a very confidential manner. The firm should be prepared to pay for the program, or at least to advance funds to ensure the lawyer's participation.

4. *Arranging for satisfactory compensation of the abusing lawyer.* The firm must recognize the financial needs of the lawyer in question. This means either full compensation or a level of compensation sufficient enough to permit the lawyer to fully focus on treatment without worrying about supporting his or her family.

5. *Arranging for client coverage.* A lawyer who is abusing drugs or alcohol cannot properly serve his or her clients, and any firm permitting an abusing lawyer to represent clients is inviting trouble. The facts and circumstances of each situation will define how best to handle the matter. In some cases, the lawyer requires full-time treatment, and other lawyers must completely take over his or her clients. In other instances, the lawyer may be able to serve clients while undergoing treatment, but the firm should ensure that there is appropriate supervision of this lawyer's work.

6. *Requiring post-treatment testing or monitoring.* Alcohol and drugs are highly addictive, and unfortunately, lawyers can successfully complete treatment programs but then relapse. Post-treatment testing or monitoring serves two important purposes. First, it is a constant reminder to the lawyer of the need to stay clean. And second, it provides the firm with the confidence that the lawyer is, in fact, staying clean.

7. *Preparing for a relapse.* The facts and circumstances of an individual case will define the firm's response. In certain situations, the lawyer should be given a second chance to re-enroll in a program. In other situations, and almost certainly in situations involving a second relapse, the firm should be prepared to part ways with the lawyer. The firm should inform the lawyer from the start that it is prepared to let him or her go if there is a relapse, which should provide the lawyer with more of an incentive to stay clean.

When all is said and done, the firm must act humanely. Yet the firm must also be true to its principles if it is to serve its clients properly and set the right example for its lawyers and staff.

Ultimately, this means adopting and adhering to a rigid program, and being fully prepared to part ways with a lawyer if this program is not being followed. As the Good Book says, sometimes one must be cruel to be merciful.

The Lawyer Who Wishes to Slow Down

Lawyers are entitled to slow down without retiring altogether, and firms should be prepared to accommodate this desire. Lawyers should not have to choose between working full-time or withdrawing from the firm.

At our firm we have adopted a "semi-retirement" policy, which provides partners with the option to stay with the firm, but with a reduced set of demands and expectations. Under our policy, a partner may elect semi-retirement beginning as early as age sixty. The firm, in turn, has no right to compel semi-retirement.

Our semi-retired partner's hour expectations are essentially cut in half and compensation is reduced, with compensation tied into the partner's overall productivity and contribution to the firm. When the contribution falls below a certain level, the partner may lose his or her vote, but is still entitled to attend and participate at our partnership meetings.

Lawyers who wish to slow down can still make important contributions to their firms in financial terms: by training and mentoring younger lawyers and passing on sage advice at partnership meetings. If firms insist that their partners all bill X number of hours, and do not allow another option for this type of lawyer, they deprive themselves of potentially valuable resources.

Dealing with a Long-Term Illness

A firm must be prepared for the long-term illness of a lawyer or staff member and should establish long-term disability insurance for the financial protection of both the individual and the firm. Beyond the insurance issue, the managing partner must be prepared to deal with several important issues.

1. *The issue of confidentiality.* The individual has a right to preserve the confidentiality of his or her medical condition, and the firm must respect this right. There may be situations in which the managing partner will be asked to keep the matter confidential from other partners. The partners should be made to understand that they might make the same request if they were in that same position.

2. *The firm must ensure appropriate coverage of the work of the individual.* This is especially critical when the ill person is a partner with a major clientele. The managing partner should work closely with that ill partner to discuss coverage and determine, what, if any, continuing supervisory role that ill partner can play.

3. *The firm must exhibit respect and sensitivity during the reintegration of the individual as he or she is recovering.* The convalescence may be a prolonged one, precluding an immediate full-time return to the demands of practice. The managing partner must take the lead in reminding partners to understand that people do not choose to be sick and that recovery from a long-term illness can take a long time. The managing partner needs to monitor the situation, but malingerers are a rarity, and the individual should be given the benefit of the doubt.

Mergers and Laterals 17

We live in an era of merger mania. Few days go by without a report on the business page of a merger involving at least one industry giant. This merger craze has also hit the legal community, especially with the proliferation of national law firms.

Lateral movement of partners from one firm to another has been commonplace for a number of years. Loyalty to one's firm means much less than it used to. Firms are also less reticent to solicit one another's partners than they were in the past.

Since the managing partner is the focal point for any consideration of mergers and laterals, he or she may wish to work with a committee on this issue. Given the sensitivity of any such discussion, and especially given the crucial nature of a decision to merge or add lateral partners, the managing partner must play an active role in guaranteeing that the process is done properly.

Mergers

Consideration of a merger is a multifaceted, time-consuming process. The managing partner can control this process by initiating discussions that proceed in phases. Before too many partners become involved in too many meetings, it is important to determine whether there is agreement in principle between the two firms on major issues such as name, space, and a philosophy regarding division of profits. These issues should be discussed at initial meetings, which should involve a few representatives from each firm. These sessions should also address whether there are major client conflict issues. Only after it is determined that there is a basis for going forward—and that there are no major stumbling blocks—should the dialog be broadened to include more of the partners from both firms.

The process should then proceed contemporaneously on two fronts. First, there should be broader discussions on issues such as goals and aspirations for the merged firm, as well as practice synergies. These "chemistry" discussions are especially important in defining whether there is personal and professional compatibility among the partners of both firms.

Second, there should be detailed "due diligence" review of the other firm. Each firm should look at information—which dates back at least three years—regarding various financial issues and review personnel developments, also from the past three years. At this time, there should be a more detailed review of client lists to spot potential conflicts. A smaller group of partners should handle the due diligence review but should fully disclose their results to all partners. During this time period, inquiry about the other firm should be made with other lawyers in the community who know that firm, including that firm's former partners.

When it is clear that significant progress is being made on both the chemistry and due diligence fronts, the managing partner should arrange for a small group from the two firms to proceed with more intensive negotiations on the various terms and conditions of the merger. A letter of intent should be prepared, which sets forth all of the major terms of the merger arrangement. Following review and consideration by the partners, the letter of intent can be signed and a detailed merger agreement drafted. The merger agreement should address the following issues:

◆ Name.
◆ Space.
◆ Governance and management.
◆ Form of new entity.
◆ Status of all personnel.
◆ Treatment of assets and liabilities.
◆ Tax issues.
◆ Integration of benefit plans.
◆ Outline of the key provisions of the partnership agreement of the merged firm.

Between the signing of the merger agreement and the effective date of the merger, a transition team should be appointed to assist in the detailed planning of the integration of virtually every aspect of the two firms. The work of the transition team should continue after the merger, since the true integration of two firms requires a good deal of time, which is absolutely necessary to an effective merger.

The managing partner needs to control the disclosure of the merger deliberations to non-partners. The initial merger discussions should be kept confidential, in the case that the two firms do not proceed with the merger, so both false hopes and fears can be avoided. Once the merger deliberations get under way, however, it is too much to expect that merger discussions can be kept totally confidential. The managing partner is best advised, once the process goes beyond the initial stage, to make some type of limited disclosure to associates and staff. People prefer to hear from the managing partner than the rumor mill, which may work its ugly ways.

As the merger negotiations progress more seriously, and when the letter of intent has been signed, associates and staff should be more fully apprised of what is going on—and hopefully reassured of their job security and the new opportunities the merger presents. The managing partner should arrange for the associates and administrative directors to meet some of the key partners of the other firm. Once the merger agreement is signed, the associates and staff should be fully involved in the integration process, meeting as many of their new colleagues as possible.

Laterals

The consideration of lateral partners involves many of the same elements of a merger consideration, but on a smaller scale. The stages of the process are similar: the initial confidential discussions, a dual track of chemistry discussions and due diligence, negotiation and execution of the contractual arrangement, and the integration process. As in a merger, the managing partner must play a key role in each stage of the process.

In the initial discussions, the firm should set up a candid discussion with the lawyer to find out why this lawyer wishes to leave his or her present employer. The firm should ask the lateral what his or her expectations are for the new firm and how the lateral's practice would be integrated into the new firm. Without necessarily revealing all of the firm's "dirty laundry," the managing partner should disclose any major problems or issues at the firm. If the potential lateral has been in solo practice and does not have much firm experience, the managing partner needs to go to greater pains to educate the lateral about the firm. Candor and disclosure should prevail over tact and politeness to avoid surprises once the lateral arrives at the firm.

The chemistry discussions and due diligence review should proceed in the same way a merger does. Chemistry is extremely important, particularly in a smaller firm. This is a two-way process: the partners need to be comfortable with the lateral, and the lateral needs to be comfortable with the firm. The lateral's position at the firm may threaten a partner or two. In this case, it is up to the managing partner to work this out with such partners, hopefully demonstrating that their practices are complemented, not threatened, by the lateral's addition.

Due diligence should definitely include checking out the lateral with members of his or her present firm. This should only be done with the lateral's consent, as the lateral may want to keep it secret that he or she is thinking of leaving. It may well be that the lateral has a confidant at the former office, who knows of the lateral's plans and could be used as a reference. At the very least, the managing partner should check any additional references at the lateral's firm once the parties are farther along in the process. A contract can be signed subject to a final reference check.

The negotiation of the lateral's contract should protect the firm's interests. A provision should be included for an amicable divorce if, at the end of a year or so, either side decides that it is not working out. The financial arrangement should provide incentives to the lateral while protecting the firm.

At our firm we have compensated laterals based upon a percentage of the work they bring into the firm (with a higher percentage for their own hours and a lower percentage for hours delegated to others) and a percentage of their production on existing clients of the firm. Following the year "look-see" period, the lateral may then be voted in as a formula partner of the firm.

The integration process of a lateral is very important. A firm should fully integrate the lateral into the relevant practice group and orient that lawyer to the firm's policies and procedures. Every effort should be made to have the lateral meet and get to know all of the partners and as many associates and staff members as possible. The managing partner should check in regularly with the lateral to confirm that the integration is proceeding well.

Controlling the Process

Where a firm is considering a merger into a national firm, the focus should not simply be on issues of compensation and profits—a number of important additional considerations come into play.

1. *Are the partners prepared to lose some of their autonomy or to become a branch office?*
2. *Will there be increased pressure to raise rates to existing clients to conform to the national firm's financial expectations?*
3. *What assurances are being given for the tenure of partners?*
4. *Will the partners have control over the clients they introduce to the firm?*
5. *What control will the firm have over the hiring and retention of its employees and staff?*
6. *Will the culture of the firm be redefined?*

A final note: sometimes the best decision is not to merge or take on the lateral. Once momentum builds in a certain direction, it is hard to stop the process without causing some disappointment among partners or embarrassment vis-à-vis associates and staff. Yet, one of the most important things a managing partner can do is control the process, so that it does not move more quickly than it should. The managing partner should know when to put the brakes on in case an important issue that could be a stumbling block to an eventual agreement arises.

PART IV

A Few Good Ideas

Rewarding Programs | **18**

It is not every new idea that leads to a successful, enduring program. It is important, however, to encourage creativity and promote new ideas. Sometimes even the simplest ideas can result in the most rewarding programs. The following are a few programs and policies we have successfully implemented at our firm, the genesis of each being a fairly simple idea.

Case Presentation Program

Several years ago, one of my partners approached me to get my thoughts on a potential contingent fee case in the intellectual property area. After hearing his description of the claim, I thought that the potential client had a decent legal basis for proceeding, but I had some doubts as to how the case would play before a jury.

I suggested that this partner and an associate working with him prepare ten-minute closing arguments for the two sides of the case and present their arguments the next day to members of our support staff, who would constitute our jury. We invited interested secretaries, administrators, and bookkeepers—strictly on a voluntary basis—to a pizza lunch in one of our conference rooms, to listen and then share their thoughts on the presentations.

Thus was born our case presentation program. We use this program for potential new cases and existing ones in which trial dates are imminent. The format we followed that first time is the format we have used ever since, in what has become a very successful monthly event.

One of our trial lawyers serves as the presiding judge, and after pizza is served and order declared, he or she briefly describes the nature of the case. Typically, our "jurors" are not familiar with which of the sides our firm is representing, or even thinking of representing. The ten-minute closing arguments are presented. The staff members are then invited to ask questions of the two lawyers to fill in the holes. The judge instructs the jurors on the basic legal issues, and asks each one to write down his or her verdict.

Because we try to complete the session in an hour, we do not allow an opportunity for a true group deliberation. We simply go around the table and ask each staff member to state his or her verdict and the basis for the decision. We then invite our presenting lawyers to ask the jurors questions to obtain additional insight into their decisions.

The program has proven to be a win-win for all concerned.

For one thing, the partner derives the benefit of how would-be jurors might think, and I can say with conviction that some very valuable and thoughtful insights are expressed at each of our sessions. It is not unusual for a partner to get too close to a case, and to focus on certain issues at the expense of others. As a result of the input from our staff members, the partner is able to focus or refocus on points that he or she overlooked.

The associate, in turn, is afforded the opportunity to prepare and present a closing argument—a very valuable experience. We typically invite interested lawyers to attend our case presentations (although not to participate as jurors), and they may also provide their thoughts as to the effectiveness of the arguments presented.

Both the partner and the associate benefit because one of them has to prepare and present the closing of the opposing side. All too often, trial lawyers become so attached to their clients' positions that they lose perspective on the strengths of the opposing party's position. The case presentation program requires that we think long and hard about the strengths of the other side.

Most important, from the standpoint of building a successful firm, the case presentation program has proven to be a winner for our staff members. Apart from a free lunch, our secretaries, bookkeepers, and administrators derive satisfaction from their thoughts and perspectives being valued—highly valued—by our lawyers. They also gain a greater appreciation of what our lawyers do, and of the types of cases in which our firm becomes involved.

I heartily recommend this program to other firms. My only admonition is that you need to keep the case presentations simple. Present the primary count of the complaint, not ten counts. Present a key defense or two, but not ten.

Discussion Groups

Our discussion group program evolved from the rather simple idea that we should promote communication among our lawyers and support staff in areas outside the law. All too often, the only interaction between lawyers and staff is in the context of client representations and work assignments. Lawyers speak on nonlegal matters to other lawyers, but rarely to staff. And secretaries and staff members are reluctant to initiate conversations with lawyers on nonlegal matters.

To promote greater interaction between lawyers and staff, we have established a monthly discussion group that is held over a bring-your-own (BYO) lunch in one of our conference rooms. Attendance is completely voluntary. We typically have five or six regular attendees, joined each session by another five or six people who have a special interest in the subject being discussed.

The subject matter of a particular session is designated ahead of time, often at the suggestion of one of the group's members. The group might discuss a reading or a recent movie. Or a discussion may address issues relating to civil rights, such as our traditional January discussion, scheduled close to Martin Luther King, Jr. Day.

The most important point of our discussion groups is that we provide a forum for our lawyers and staff to interact in ways they would not otherwise. We learn more about one another and develop a greater personal respect and appreciation for those with whom we work.

And we have a good time.

Client Roundtable Program

Lawyers tend to think of their individual clients quite narrowly, focusing on the particular representation and fee arrangement. Yet we are in a position to assist our clients beyond the four corners of individual representation. After all, many of our clients are in business and consistently looking for ways to increase their sales and productivity. As lawyers, we can help our clients by simply introducing them to other clients.

Our client roundtables start off when we invite a group of clients to a breakfast meeting. Each roundtable is attended by eight-to-ten clients and around four lawyers, who represent several of our departments. We lead off the session by asking clients to take five minutes to introduce themselves and their businesses and their number one business concern. The ensuing discussion may proceed in any one of a number of directions. Our experience is that there are fascinating synergies between and among our clients. Ideas and suggestions are passed from one client to another. Marketing leads are offered. Common experiences are shared. And, if nothing else, our clients appreciate the opportunity to learn more about other businesses and industries.

We adjourn each session after an hour and a half but keep the conference room available for informal discussions among individual clients and our lawyers. It is not unusual to walk by the conference room a half hour later and see clients engrossed in conversation.

Our clients and our lawyers benefit from the roundtables. By listening to our clients' issues, we become more attuned to their legal needs. We also enhance our understanding of various industries. And while we make sure that the lawyers do not dominate the sessions, we may offer a few good words of advice here and there, demonstrating our expertise to the clients. The clients truly appreciate receiving the free legal advice.

We may announce ahead of time that the session will focus on a particular subject, such as corporate finance or employee relations, but we have just as much success when we do not have a particular theme.

Marketing Meetings

Like most law firms, we have devoted increased resources over the past several years to "practice development," a euphemism for marketing. We developed a firm brochure and Web page, sponsor seminars, and encourage our lawyers to become published. Ultimately, we have recognized that our most effective marketing tool is to provide quality service and results to our clients, as most of our new work is generated from existing and new clients who are referred to us by present clients.

As an additional tool in our practice development arena, we have instituted a bi-weekly marketing luncheon. The firm encourages all of our lawyers to attend these luncheons and expects them to attend at least one of the two sessions each month.

Each marketing meeting consists of informal presentations by approximately five or six lawyers, who hopefully represent at least several of our practice groups. Each presenting lawyer describes a new representation, explains how that client came to retain us, and summarizes its legal problem. At the conclusion of each presentation, we open up the floor for questions and comments.

We have found that these sessions accomplish three major purposes, all of which support the overall marketing effort of the firm.

1. *The sessions serve to educate our lawyers about the areas of expertise and types of practices of the other lawyers in the firm.* This shared knowledge also permits our lawyers to gain a greater sensitivity into the potential needs of their clients in other practice areas. Our lawyers can then let their clients know that there are other lawyers in our firm who are able to handle their special needs.

2. *The sessions serve as a training ground for our younger lawyers,* who learn how clients have come into the firm, and what marketing was done to attract them.

3. *The presenting lawyer often receives input from others in the room as to the substance of the client's legal issue.* Others offer some very thoughtful suggestions to the presenting lawyer as to how he or she might follow up in addressing the client's issue.

You can see that we order in a fair amount of food at our firm. If the availability of free pizza or deli sandwiches induces a few additional people to attend these types of sessions, it is well worth it, because these programs work.

Sabbatical Program

A few years ago I introduced the idea of a sabbatical program at a partnership retreat. The overall response was predictable—partners resisted the notion based upon financial objections. I figured that I would raise the issue again at a later time, perhaps a year or two down the road. What happened instead was that one of my partners re-raised the issue on his own a few months after the retreat. He requested to take a sabbatical along the lines of the program I presented.

The partner in question was a perfect candidate for a sabbatical. He had been practicing for twenty-five years, fifteen with our firm, and had spent the two most recent years representing one side of a family in a very complicated intra-family commercial real estate dispute. The representation had been extremely time-consuming and quite stressful. Thankfully—largely due to the efforts of this particular partner—a successful resolution was achieved. I was quite pleased that the request was coming from this particular partner. He fully deserved and needed a sabbatical, and his example would allow me to demonstrate to our remaining partners that the program could work.

Our partners approved the request, albeit reluctantly. The partner in question went sailing for six months, returned to the firm refreshed and with his client base fully intact. The program worked.

Our sabbatical program permits partners who have been with the firm ten years or more to take six months away from the firm, for any purpose at all. The program is completely voluntarily. While away, the partner should have as little contact as possible with the firm or his or her clients, except in the event of a real emergency. Planning is to be done up front to ensure the effective transitioning and coverage of client matters. Clients are immediately told what is going on.

The sabbatical is effectively financed 40 percent by the partner and 60 percent by the firm, based on our formula for the division of profits, which provides for three-year averaging of production and delegation credits. The partner on sabbatical does not pick up production credits during the six months (assuming he or she is truly on sabbatical) but has the benefit of two-and-one-half years of production credits already in place under the formula. The partner's share of the production pool should only be reduced by one sixth. This reduction will carry over for the next two years, but this means that the partner's effective monetary contribution to his or her sabbatical will be spread out over three years. To ensure proper coverage for clients, the partner on sabbatical should experience an increase in delegation credits—as other lawyers will take on his or her clients' work—and the spike in delegation credits would also carry over for the next two years, mitigating lost production credits to some extent.

The bottom line is that if there is appropriate client coverage, there is no significant impact on the finances of the firm, or the take-home of the partner on sabbatical.

Why should firms consider this type of program? There are, in fact, a number of potential benefits.

1. *A sabbatical program permits lawyers to avoid burnout, and could easily result in the lengthening of overall careers.* This was certainly the case with our partner.
2. *A sabbatical program permits lawyers to expand their horizons.* The six months might be spent travelling, teaching, studying, writing, doing pro bono work, or serving with a

governmental agency. Even if a partner chooses to sail for six months, his or her horizons are certainly expanded. He or she experiences a challenge, enjoys and confronts nature, and takes the time for reading and introspection.

3. *A sabbatical may provide wonderful marketing opportunities,* helping the individual partner and also potentially enhancing the firm.

4. *A well-planned sabbatical program affords an opportunity for younger lawyers to step up to the plate* when taking on the increased responsibilities that serving the clients of the partner on sabbatical entails.

5. *A sabbatical program may enhance a firm's recruitment efforts.*

Although we have not done so as of yet, there is no reason why firms should not also adopt programs permitting their more tenured staff to take mini-sabbaticals, perhaps for a three-month duration. Secretaries and paralegals also endure burnout, and could certainly benefit from a mini-sabbatical. If they benefit, so does the firm in the long run. A staff sabbatical program may also increase long-term loyalty, both from staff members who have taken sabbaticals and staff members anticipating their own. Such a program could also easily enhance the firm's recruitment efforts.

Conclusion

A law firm is composed of partners, associates, administrators, and staff members. If the managing partner's job can be summed up in one phrase, it is to "add value to the firm so that the whole of the firm is greater than the sum of its parts."

◆ By formulating a coherent strategic plan and defining appropriate firm-wide and individual goals, the managing partner can encourage the firm and its lawyers to reach higher than they may have otherwise.

◆ By establishing the proper governance, management, and committee structure, the managing partner can do a great deal to promote personal interaction that permits people to work with and not against each other.

◆ By coordinating the activities of the various practice groups, promoting high standards of practice and service, and attracting strong legal talent to the firm, the managing partner can enhance the synergistic efforts of the firm's lawyers.

◆ By promoting a healthy working atmosphere, implementing rational policies and procedures, and initiating creative programs, the managing partner can evoke the best efforts of the firm's personnel.

Poor management, on the other hand, will ensure that the whole will not come close to the sum of the parts. If partners are bickering with one another, and if associates and staff are unhappy and leaving the firm, clients will not be properly served and the firm will suffer.

Finally, a word about succession: the managing partner will eventually want to step down from the position but must be responsible for making sure that succession goes smoothly. The ideal model is to have a managing-partner elect in place a full year before the managing partner steps down, so that the managing partner-elect may experience every facet of the position. The departing managing partner should turn over outlines of responsibilities and management files, but there is no substitute for firsthand experience. By leading the firm with the managing partner, the managing partner-elect can gain valuable experience and obtain the managing partner's sage advice as events are taking place.

Appendix: The Client's Bill of Rights

As discussed in the preamble, legal ethical standards define in some detail the obligations of lawyers to clients, but there are a number of voids. Firms should consider adopting a "Client's Bill of Rights" to codify those basic rights to which any client should be entitled. Although these rights extend beyond what a firm is ethically obligated to provide, the firm that formally adopts a Client's Bill of Rights may find that it is able to attract and retain more clients. Even if it does not wish to formally adopt this bill of rights, the firm should at least informally recognize the basic rights of their clients. The firm should also instill in their lawyers a sense of what is required to ensure that the clients will have the benefit of these rights.

The Client's Bill of Rights should include the following ten entitlements.

The Right to Informed Consent

The doctrine of informed consent is well established in the medical arena—well known to not only medical malpractice lawyers but all lawyers as well. Lawyers need to recognize that clients are also fully entitled to an informed consent in the legal arena. This means that the client is fully informed of the pros and cons, the upside potential and downside risk, and the anticipated cost of each alternative.

Prior to presenting these alternatives, a lawyer must have a full understanding of a client's issues in the broader context, which includes the applicable legal principles, the factual background, the relevant business and industry considerations, and the anticipated response of the opposing party.

The client's right to an informed consent is continuous in nature. Most client representations are quite fluid, with developments and changes in the overall context of the case. The client is entitled to a full review of options as the circumstances change.

One other comment related to informed consent: the lawyer has the responsibility to be objective, to inform the client when the client is wrong or seeking a position that is factually or legally untenable. Sometimes it is not easy to tell a client that he or she is wrong—a lawyer may risk termination when blunt with a client. Yet informed consent requires an open and honest evaluation of the matter, and if honesty means bad news for the client, so be it.

The Right to Independent Representation

The client has the right to independent representation, with counsel acting free of legal ethical conflicts and business conflicts as well. The disciplinary rules are quite explicit as to what constitutes a conflict of interest from a legal standpoint. In contrast, there are no clear rules with respect to conflicts arising from the business standpoint. Firms often represent business competitors, and in many cases, this presents no real problem. But when representation of one client is to the business disadvantage of another, or when loyalty to one client precludes the lawyer from providing zealous representation to another client who is a competitor of the first, a potential business conflict arises. Clients have the right to full disclosure to possible business conflicts, just as they are entitled to full disclosure of a legal conflict.

The Right to Competent Representation

A client obviously has the right to competent representation. This means that a lawyer must possess a comprehensive understanding of the client's goals, the legal and factual issues at hand, and the ability to achieve the desired result. A lawyer has the obligation to inform a prospective client if he or she cannot muster the means for providing competent representation. This is not easy for a lawyer to do, especially if the lawyer is looking to attract work. Even more difficult is the situation in which the lawyer initially believes that he or she has the expertise but realizes after the representation has begun that this is not the case. That lawyer must either bring in additional help, with disclosure to the client, or work with the client to transition the matter to competent successor counsel.

The Right to Quality Service

In the preamble, I defined the elements of good service: communication, responsiveness, and timeliness. A key point for a lawyer to remember is that what may be routine and humdrum for the lawyer is of critical importance to the client. A litigation lawyer may be handling fifty cases at one time, and perhaps Client X's case is the least interesting. Yet for Client X, this is the only litigation in which it is involved, and Client X cares very much about what is going on in the case.

The Right of Access to the Originating Lawyer/Supervising Expert/Managing Partner

A client with a litigation matter contacts Partner A, it's outside corporate counsel, and Partner A refers the matter to a litigation partner, Partner B. Partner B then assigns the matter to Associate, who has a primary responsibility for handling the matter. This is a very typical case scenario. What is unfortunately all too common, however, is that the client is not able to access anyone at the firm about the litigation other than Associate. Partner A and Partner B won't return calls from the client, or they have Associate return the calls for them.

A client has the right to access the originating lawyer, and the client has the right to access the expertise supervisor. The client should also have the right of access to the firm's managing partner to present any issue that cannot be resolved with any of the other three lawyers.

The Right to Have Confidences Preserved

The legal ethical rules impose strict guidelines for the preservation of client confidences. Most lawyers take these obligations quite seriously. Where firms fall short is in failing to inculcate among staff members the importance of preserving client confidences. Firms must be vigilant in training staff members to understand that they should not be divulging client confidences outside of the office.

The Right to Fairness in Billing

While the disciplinary rules preclude a lawyer from charging an excessive fee, the client is entitled to something more than simply the right to be billed a nonexcessive fee. The client is entitled to overall fairness in billing. Fairness in billing requires the following:

◆ Posting of time charges that reflect work performed on an efficient basis.
◆ No padding of hours.
◆ Avoiding unnecessary multiple teaming.
◆ Billing disbursements at cost.
◆ Respecting the client's budgetary constraints.
◆ Honoring estimates provided up front, or otherwise justifying why the bill exceeded the estimate.

The Right to Terminate the Relationship

The client has the right to terminate its relationship with a lawyer at any time and for any reason. Obviously the lawyer may have a legitimate claim for payment of services rendered through the termination, but the lawyer has no right to compel a client to continue representation.

The Right to Not Have Its Position Compromised by the Actions of the Lawyer

Apart from the lawyer's duty to competently represent the client, the lawyer has the additional duty of avoiding any action that might compromise the client's position. For example, if a lawyer has acted well within the disciplinary strictures defining the publicity about a case, but the client wished to avoid any publicity, the lawyer has committed a disservice to that client by going public. And when a lawyer's aggressive conduct in a business negotiation results in the capitulation by the other side on a particular point—but also results in long-term harm to the parties' business relationship—the lawyer also has performed a disservice.

The Right to Know What Went Wrong

Sometimes, things do not work out according to plan, and the lawyer is unable to meet the client's goals. Or perhaps victory was achieved but the victory was a Pyrrhic one. The client is entitled to full candor from the lawyer about what went wrong and why. Lawyers can make mistakes, and it is the responsibility of the lawyer to own up to any errors. If it means that the client may have potential recourse against the lawyer, so be it.

I look forward to the day when most firms acknowledge that their clients are entitled to these rights. Who knows, we may even find that the public's current perception of the bar will dramatically improve.

Selected Resources from the ABA Law Practice Management Section

Compensation Plans for Law Firms, Third Edition
  Edited by James D. Cotterman, 2001

The Complete Internet Handbook for Lawyers
  Jerry Lawson, 1999

Connecting with Your Client: Success through Improved Client Communications Techniques
  Noelle C. Nelson, 1996

Easy Self-Audits for the Busy Law Office
  Nancy Byerly Jones, 1999

Handling Personnel Issues
  Francis T. Coleman and Douglas Rosenfeld, 1997

Keeping Good Lawyers: Best Practices to Create Career Satisfaction
  M. Diane Vogt and Lori-Ann Rickard, 2000

Law Office Policy and Procedures Manual, Fourth Edition
  Robert C. Wert and Howard I. Hatoff, 2000

*Law Office Procedures Manual for Solos and Small Firms,
Second Edition*
   Demetrios Dimitriou, 2000

The Lawyer's Guide to Balancing Life and Work
   George W. Kaufman, 1999

Strengthening Your Firm: Strategies for Success
   Edited by Arthur Greene, 1997

Telecommuting for Lawyers
   Nicole Belson Goluboff, 1998

Index

About the Author

Lawrence G. Green served as Managing Partner of Perkins, Smith & Cohen, LLP in Boston for ten years. An honors graduate of Wesleyan University, Mr. Green received his Juris Doctor from New York University School of Law, where he was a Root-Tilden Scholar. Mr. Green has served as President of the Wesleyan Alumni Association of Greater Boston, and as President of the N.Y.U. Law Alumni of New England. He is the President of the American Jewish Society for Service. Mr. Green specializes in the areas of business litigation, antitrust and creditors rights, and has lectured before bar and business groups in these areas.

Law Firm Partnership Guide: Strengthening Your Firm. Addresses what to do after your firm is up and running, including how to handle: change, financial problems, governance issues, compensating firm owners, and leadership.

Law Law Law on the Internet. Presents the most influential law-related Web sites. Features Web site reviews of the *National Law Journal's 250*, so you can save time surfing the Net and quickly find the information you need.

Law Office Policy and Procedures Manual, 4th Ed. A model for law office policies and procedures (includes diskette). Covers law office organization, management, personnel policies, financial management, technology, and communications systems.

Law Office Staff Manual for Solos and Small Firms. Use this manual as is or customize it using the book's diskette. Includes general office policies on confidentiality, employee compensation, sick leave, sexual harassment, billing, and more.

The Lawyer's Guide to Creating Web Pages. A practical guide that clearly explains HTML, covers how to design a Web site, and introduces Web-authoring tools.

The Lawyer's Guide to the Internet. A guide to what the Internet is (and isn't), how it applies to the legal profession, and the different ways it can—and should—be used.

The Lawyer's Guide to Marketing on the Internet. This book talks about the pluses and minuses of marketing on the Internet, as well as how to develop an Internet marketing plan.

The Lawyer's Quick Guide to E-Mail. Covers basic and intermediate topics, including setting up an e-mail program, sending messages, managing received messages, using mailing lists, security, and more.

The Lawyer's Quick Guide to Microsoft® Internet Explorer; The Lawyer's Quick Guide to Netscape® Navigator. These two guides de-mystify the most popular Internet browsers. Four quick and easy lessons include: Basic Navigation, Setting a Bookmark, Browsing with a Purpose, and Keeping What You Find.

The Lawyer's Quick Guide to Timeslips®. Filled with practical examples, this guide uses three short, interactive lessons to show to efficiently use Timeslips.

The Lawyer's Quick Guide to WordPerfect® 7.0/8.0 for Windows®. Covers multitasking, entering and editing text, formatting letters, creating briefs, and more. Includes a diskette with practice exercises and word templates.

Leaders' Digest: A Review of the Best Books on Leadership. This book will help you find the best books on leadership to help you achieve extraordinary and exceptional leadership skills.

Living with the Law: Strategies to Avoid Burnout and Create Balance. Examines ways to manage stress, make the practice of law more satisfying, and improve client service.

Marketing Success Stories. This collection of anecdotes provides an inside look at how successful lawyers market themselves, their practice specialties, their firms, and their profession.

Microsoft® Word for Windows® in One Hour for Lawyers. Uses four easy lessons to help you prepare, save, and edit a basic document in Word.

Practicing Law Without Clients: Making a Living as a Freelance Lawyer. Describes freelance legal researching, writing, and consulting opportunities that are available to lawyers.

Quicken® in One Hour for Lawyers. With quick, concise instructions, this book explains the basics of Quicken and how to use the program to detect and analyze financial problems.

Risk Management. Presents practical ways to asses your level of risk, improve client services, and avoid mistakes that can lead to costly malpractice claims, civil liability, or discipline. Includes Law Firm Quality/In Control (QUIC) Surveys on diskette and other tools to help you perform a self-audit.

Running a Law Practice on a Shoestring. Offers a crash course in successful entrepreneurship. Features money-saving tips on office space, computer equipment, travel, furniture, staffing, and more.

Successful Client Newsletters. Written for lawyers, editors, writers, and marketers, this book can help you start a newsletter from scratch, redesign an existing one, or improve your current practices in design, production, and marketing.

Survival Guide for Road Warriors. A guide to using a notebook computer (laptop) and other technology to improve your productivity in your office, on the road, in the courtroom, or at home.

Telecommuting for Lawyers. Discover methods for implementing a successful telecommuting program that can lead to increased productivity, improved work product, higher revenues, lower overhead costs, and better communications. Addressing both law firms and telecommuters, this guide covers start-up, budgeting, setting policies, selecting participants, training, and technology.

Through the Client's Eyes. Includes an overview of client relations and sample letters, surveys, and self-assessment questions to gauge your client relations acumen.

Time Matters® in One Hour for Lawyers. Employs quick, easy lessons to show you how to: add contacts, cases, and notes to Time Matters; work with events and the calendar; and integrate your data into a case management system that suits your needs.

Wills, Trusts, and Technology. Reveals why you should automate your estates practice; identifies what should be automated; explains how to select the right software; and helps you get up and running with the software you select.

Win-Win Billing Strategies. Prepared by a blue-ribbon ABA task force of practicing lawyers, corporate counsel, and management consultants, this book explores what constitutes "value" and how to bill for it. You'll understand how to get fair compensation for your work and communicate and justify fees to cost-conscious clients.

Women Rainmakers' 101+ Best Marketing Tips. A collection of over 130 marketing from women rainmakers throughout the country. Features tips on image, networking, public relations, and advertising.

Year 2000 Problem and the Legal Profession. In clear, nontechnical terms, this book will help you identify, address, and meet the challenges that Y2K poses to the legal industry.

Order Form

Qty	Title	LPM Price	Regular Price	Total
_____	ABA Guide to International Business Negotiations (5110331)	$ 74.95	$ 84.95	$_____
_____	ABA Guide to Lawyer Trust Accounts (5110374)	69.95	79.95	$_____
_____	ABA Guide to Legal Marketing (5110341)	69.95	79.95	$_____
_____	ABA Guide to Prof. Managers in the Law Office (5110373)	69.95	79.95	$_____
_____	Anatomy of a Law Firm Merger, Second Edition (5110434)	74.95	89.95	$_____
_____	Billing Innovations (5110366)	124.95	144.95	$_____
_____	Changing Jobs, 3rd Ed.		*please call for information*	$_____
_____	Compensation Plans for Lawyers, 3rd Ed. (5110452)	84.95	99.95	$_____
_____	Complete Guide to Marketing Your Law Practice (5110428)	74.95	89.95	$_____
_____	Complete Internet Handbook for Lawyers (5110413)	39.95	49.95	$_____
_____	Computerized Case Management Systems (5110409)	39.95	49.95	$_____
_____	Connecting with Your Client (5110378)	54.95	64.95	$_____
_____	Do-It-Yourself Public Relations (5110352)	69.95	79.95	$_____
_____	Easy Self Audits for the Busy Law Firm		*please call for information*	$_____
_____	Finding the Right Lawyer (5110339)	14.95	14.95	$_____
_____	Flying Solo, 2nd Ed. (5110328)	29.95	34.95	$_____
_____	Handling Personnel Issues in the Law Office (5110381)	59.95	69.95	$_____
_____	HotDocs® in One Hour for Lawyers (5110403)	29.95	34.95	$_____
_____	How to Build and Manage an Employment Law Practice (5110389)	44.95	54.95	$_____
_____	How to Build and Manage an Estates Law Practice		*please call for information*	$_____
_____	How to Build and Manage a Personal Injury Practice (5110386)	44.95	54.95	$_____
_____	How to Draft Bills Clients Rush to Pay (5110344)	39.95	49.95	$_____
_____	How to Start & Build a Law Practice, Millennium Fourth Edition (5110415)	47.95	54.95	$_____
_____	Internet Fact Finder for Lawyers (5110399)	34.95	39.95	$_____
_____	Law Firm Partnership Guide: Getting Started (5110363)	64.95	74.95	$_____
_____	Law Firm Partnership Guide: Strengthening Your Firm (5110391)	64.95	74.95	$_____
_____	Law Law Law on the Internet (5110400)	34.95	39.95	$_____
_____	Law Office Policy & Procedures Manual, 4th Ed. (5110441)	99.95	119.95	$_____
_____	Law Office Staff Manual for Solos & Small Firms (5110445)	59.95	69.95	$_____
_____	Lawyer's Guide to Creating Web Pages (5110383)	54.95	64.95	$_____
_____	Lawyer's Guide to the Internet (5110343)	24.95	29.95	$_____
_____	Lawyer's Guide to Marketing on the Internet (5110371)	54.95	64.95	$_____
_____	Lawyer's Quick Guide to E-Mail (5110406)	34.95	39.95	$_____
_____	Lawyer's Quick Guide to Microsoft Internet® Explorer (5110392)	24.95	29.95	$_____
_____	Lawyer's Quick Guide to Netscape® Navigator (5110384)	24.95	29.95	$_____
_____	Lawyer's Quick Guide to Timeslips® (5110405)	34.95	39.95	$_____
_____	Lawyer's Quick Guide to WordPerfect® 7.0/8.0 (5110395)	34.95	39.95	$_____
_____	Leaders' Digest (5110356)	49.95	59.95	$_____
_____	Living with the Law (5110379)	59.95	69.95	$_____
_____	Marketing Success Stories (5110382)	79.95	89.95	$_____
_____	Microsoft® Word for Windows® in One Hour for Lawyers (5110358)	19.95	29.95	$_____
_____	Practicing Law Without Clients (5110376)	49.95	59.95	$_____
_____	Quicken® in One Hour for Lawyers (5110380)	19.95	29.95	$_____
_____	Risk Management (5610123)	69.95	79.95	$_____
_____	Running a Law Practice on a Shoestring (5110387)	39.95	49.95	$_____
_____	Successful Client Newsletters (5110396)	39.95	44.95	$_____
_____	Survival Guide for Road Warriors (5110362)	24.95	29.95	$_____
_____	Telecommuting for Lawyers (5110401)	39.95	49.95	$_____
_____	Through the Client's Eyes (5110337)	69.95	79.95	$_____
_____	Time Matters® in One Hour for Lawyers (5110402)	29.95	34.95	$_____
_____	Wills, Trusts, and Technology (5430377)	74.95	84.95	$_____
_____	Win-Win Billing Strategies (5110304)	89.95	99.95	$_____
_____	Women Rainmakers' 101+ Best Marketing Tips (5110336)	14.95	19.95	$_____
_____	Year 2000 Problem and the Legal Profession (5110410)	24.95	29.95	$_____

*Handling	****Tax**	Subtotal $_____
$10.00-$24.99................\$3.95	DC residents add 5.75%	***Handling** $_____
$25.00-$49.99................\$4.95	IL residents add 8.75%	****Tax** $_____
$50.00+ \$5.95	MD residents add 5%	**TOTAL** $_____

PAYMENT
☐ Check enclosed (to the ABA) ☐ Bill Me
☐ Visa   ☐ MasterCard   ☐ American Express

_____
Account Number   Exp. Date   Signature

Name _____ Firm _____

Address _____

City _____ State _____ Zip _____

Phone Number _____ E-Mail Address _____

Mail: ABA Publication Orders, P.O. Box 10892, Chicago, Illinois 60610-0892 ♦ Phone: (800) 285-2221 ♦ FAX: (312) 988-5568

E-Mail: abasvcctr@abanet.org ♦ Internet: http://www.abanet.org/lpm/catalo

 THE SECTION OF
LAW PRACTICE
MANAGEMENT

CUSTOMER COMMENT FORM

Title of Book:_____

We've tried to make this publication as useful, accurate, and readable as possible. Please take 5 minutes to tell us if we succeeded. Your comments and suggestions will help us improve our publications. Thank you!

1. How did you acquire this publication:

☐ by mail order   ☐ at a meeting/convention   ☐ as a gift

☐ by phone order   ☐ at a bookstore   ☐ don't know

☐ other: (describe) _____

Please rate this publication as follows:

	Excellent	Good	Fair	Poor	Not Applicable
Readability: Was the book easy to read and understand?	☐	☐	☐	☐	☐
Examples/Cases: Were they helpful, practical? Were there enough?	☐	☐	☐	☐	☐
Content: Did the book meet your expectations? Did it cover the subject adequately?	☐	☐	☐	☐	☐
Organization and clarity: Was the sequence of text logical? Was it easy to find what you wanted to know?	☐	☐	☐	☐	☐
Illustrations/forms/checklists: Were they clear and useful? Were there enough?	☐	☐	☐	☐	☐
Physical attractiveness: What did you think of the appearance of the publication (typesetting, printing, etc.)?	☐	☐	☐	☐	☐

Would you recommend this book to another attorney/administrator? ☐ Yes ☐ No

How could this publication be improved? What else would you like to see in it?

_____

_____

_____

Do you have other comments or suggestions? _____

_____

_____

Name _____

Firm/Company _____

Address _____

City/State/Zip _____

Phone _____

Firm Size: _____ Area of specialization: _____

We appreciate your time and help.

Fold

BUSINESS REPLY MAIL
FIRST CLASS   PERMIT NO. 16471   CHICAGO, ILLINOIS

POSTAGE WILL BE PAID BY ADDRESSEE

AMERICAN BAR ASSOCIATION
PPM, 8th FLOOR
750 N. LAKE SHORE DRIVE
CHICAGO, ILLINOIS 60611-9851

Fold

AMERICAN BAR ASSOCIATION

Membership Application

Law Practice Management Section

Access to all these information resources and discounts – for just $3.33 a month!

Membership dues are just $40 a year – just $3.33 a month.
You probably spend more on your general business magazines and newspapers.
But they can't help you succeed in building and managing your practice
like a membership in the ABA Law Practice Management Section.
Make a small investment in success. Join today!

☑ **Yes!** I want to join the ABA Section of Law Practice Management Section and gain access to information helping me add more clients, retain and expand business with current clients, and run my law practice more efficiently and competitively!

Check the dues that apply to you:
❏ $40 for ABA members ❏ $5 for ABA Law Student Division members

Choose your method of payment:
❏ Check enclosed (make payable to American Bar Association)
❏ Bill me
❏ Charge to my: ❏ VISA® ❏ MASTERCARD® ❏ AMEX®

Card No.: _____ Exp. Date: _____

Signature: _____ Date: _____

ABA I.D.*: _____
(• *Please note: Membership in ABA is a prerequisite to enroll in ABA Sections.*)

Name: _____

Firm/Organization: _____

Address: _____

City/State/ZIP: _____

Telephone No.: _____ Fax No.: _____

Primary Email Address: _____

Get Ahead. 🏃

**Save time
by Faxing
or Phoning!**

AMERICAN BAR ASSOCIATION

ABA Law Practice Management Section

750 N. LAKE SHORE DRIVE
CHICAGO, IL 60611
PHONE: (312) 988-5619
FAX: (312) 988-5820
Email: lpm@abanet.org

▶ Fax your application to: (312) 988-5820
▶ Join by phone if using a credit card: (800) 285-2221 (ABA1)
▶ Email us for more information at: lpm@abanet.org
▶ Check us out on the Internet: http://www.abanet.org/lpm

I understand that Section dues include a $24 basic subscription to Law Practice Management; this subscription charge is not deductible from the dues and additional subscriptions are not available at this rate. Membership dues in the American Bar Association are not deductible as charitable contributions for income tax purposes. However, such dues may be deductible as a business expense.